HOMOSEXUALITY
AND THE
WESTERN CHRISTIAN
TRADITION

BY

DERRICK SHERWIN BAILEY, Ph.D.

ARCHON BOOKS
1975

Library of Congress Cataloging in Publication Data

Bailey, Derrick Sherwin, 1910-
  Homosexuality and the Western Christian tradition.

  Reprint of the 1955 ed. published by Longmans, Green,
London.
  Includes index.
  1. Homosexuality. I. Title.
HQ76.B3 1975   301.41′57   75-34384
ISBN 0-208-01492-6

First published 1955 by
LONGMANS, GREEN AND CO., LTD., London
Reprinted with permission 1975 in an unaltered and unabridged
edition as an Archon Book, an imprint of
THE SHOE STRING PRESS, INC.,
Hamden, Connecticut 06514

Printed in the United States of America

CONTENTS

v

INTRODUCTION

As a member of a small informal group of Anglican clergymen and doctors who have been studying homosexuality, and whose findings were published in a Report entitled *The Problem of Homosexuality*,[1] I undertook to investigate the Biblical and historical material bearing upon the subject. This essay is the result of some of my researches, and its scope is strictly limited by the fact that I set out to study only those factors which have helped to mould the attitude to homosexuality expressed in our present laws and public opinion. I have included nothing but what relates to the formation of the tradition of the Christian West, and this will explain certain omissions.

I have not mentioned the large and interesting mass of evidence which anthropologists have accumulated, since it chiefly concerns other peoples and cultures than those which have contributed to the making of our tradition, and does not adequately account for our particular sanctions and prejudices. Nor have I paid any regard to anecdote, pornography, and modern literature, which have at best a doubtful historical value. It may surprise the reader, however, to find that I have ignored the *paiderastia* of the Greeks— but our laws and social attitudes afford overwhelming proof that they have not been influenced in the slightest by the so-called "homosexuality" of Hellas. There is need for a thorough and unprejudiced study of this subject, and its relevance (if any) to the problems which now confront us.

My object has been simply to state as accurately and to examine as fully as possible the Biblical and ecclesiastical attitudes to homosexual practice, and the contributions of Roman law and mediæval thought to the views which are now current in the West.

---

[1] Produced for the Church of England Moral Welfare Council by the Church Information Board [1954].

I have not carried this general account beyond the end of the
Middle Ages because it does not appear that the tradition has
undergone any significant alteration since that time—although
various legal and other modifications have occurred which have
affected judicial practice and, to a limited extent, public opinion.
But having particularly in mind the situation in Britain, I have
added a chapter on the English law.

Since this is mainly an historical study, I have refrained from
any discussion of the theological and moral aspects of homosexuality, and of the morality of homosexual acts between males
in particular. Both these questions require investigation, and the
latter is but one aspect of the general morality of sexual acts—
a subject which urgently needs expert and open-minded examination. In dealing with male homosexual practices I have permitted
myself no reflections such as might have detracted from the
strictly objective and impartial presentation which is demanded.

It is clearly of the utmost importance that those who are charged
with the administration of the law, those who are being pressed
to make changes therein, and all who are concerned with the well-
being of society and the maintenance of moral standards, should
understand how the Western attitude to homosexual practices
originated and developed. If it could be shown that this attitude is
based upon presuppositions, some of which are now untenable,
the case in favour of legal reform would be strengthened, and
public opinion might become more sympathetic and enlightened.
Lately, for instance, responsible persons have alluded to "the vices
of Sodom and Gomorrah" now rampant in our midst, confidently
assuming that those vices were homosexual; but I have shown in
this essay that such an assumption is quite unfounded, and its
implications therefore irrelevant.

An historical approach is important for other reasons. In the
pages which follow it has been necessary to correct a regrettably
large number of statements made by earlier writers. Not a few of
these statements reflect adversely upon the Church; and it is
noticeable that those who demand justice and sympathy for the
homosexual frequently attribute his treatment by society and the

law to malign and obscurantist ecclesiastical influences. The Church is discredited, occasionally by an inexcusable error of fact, but far more often by some exaggerated or tendentious assertion which soon comes to be accepted as sober truth. No doubt authors such as Havelock Ellis and Westermarck (to mention only two) did not set out to denigrate the Church by a deliberate manipulation or suppression of evidence. But I think it is true to say that the anti-ecclesiastical, and sometimes anti-Christian prejudice which unfortunately seems to have animated so many writers on sexual topics inclined them to attribute instinctively to the Church every idea or development of which they disapproved. Behind any step which they chose to regard as retrogressive, any coercive law or action, any tendency towards what was to them a repressive morality, they traced the influence of the religion which they disliked but did not understand.

Let me at once make it clear that the Church cannot be exonerated from all responsibility for our present attitude to the homosexual and his problems, and for the severe penalties with which the law requites him for his offences. This responsibility, however, the Church does not bear alone; it is not as if, throughout the last two millennia, reluctant legislatures had been forced by the spiritual authority to enact laws and to prescribe punishments which they secretly detested. The Church taught and people universally believed, on what was held to be excellent authority, that homosexual practices had brought a terrible Divine vengeance upon the city of Sodom, and that the repetition of such "offences against nature" had from time to time provoked similar visitations in the form of earthquake and famine. It was understandable, therefore, that by means both of ecclesiastical discipline and of the restraints and penalties of the civil law, steps should be taken to ward off the wrath of God which might be displayed against the *filii diffidentiæ*.

Such punitive measures may not be justified either by accurate exegesis or by our insights into the causes and nature of the condition of inversion, and their continuance may rightly be regarded as unjust and lacking in humanity; but we must refrain from judging other times by the most enlightened standards of our own. In the Middle Ages ecclesiastic and layman, Church and State, were in principle unanimous, not only about the recompense meet for indulgence in homosexual practices, but also about the punishment merited by heretics, sorcerers, and witches, and the treatment appropriate to Jews. We rightly deplore such intolerance, and the dreadful consequences to which it sometimes led—but we do not always make the effort to understand an attitude of mind so different from our own in many respects. This failure of imagination is conspicuously displayed by some of the class of writer to which I have referred, but it cannot be pleaded as an excuse for the falsification of history. I shall hope to show that the legend of the "persecution" of the homosexual by the Church is a gross and unwarranted exaggeration, and that the picture of warped and narrow-minded clerics, obsessed with a horror of sodomy, delivering hordes of innocuous inverts to the *vindices flammæ* is largely a ludicrous invention of modern rationalism. Indeed, there is much to indicate that by retaining in its hands the spiritual punishment of the sodomist, the Church actually shielded him from the penalties of the secular power.

In dealing with this subject an accurate terminology is necessary. Strictly speaking, the Bible and Christian tradition know nothing of *homosexuality*; both are concerned solely with the commission of homosexual *acts*—hence the title of this study is loosely, though conveniently, worded. Homosexuality is not, as commonly supposed, a kind of *conduct*; it simply denotes in male or female a *condition* characterized by an emotional and physico-sexual propensity towards others of the same sex. As yet, we know little about the causes and nature of this condition. In many cases there are indications that it is a psychological state, due to relational maladjustments affecting the subject in the early years of childhood—though the condition may not manifest itself in any recognisable form until adolescence or later, and may even remain more or less latent throughout life. Sometimes, however, it appears to be innate, and possibly biological in origin; and some hold that it may also be hereditary. No doubt it may occasionally be due to a combination of such causes. Experience up to the present has shown that the homosexual condition is usually, for various reasons, unalterable (though some experts are more sanguine than others about the possibility of "cures"); but the compulsive physical urges often associated with it may be relieved by psychiatrical or other medical treatment.

It is important to understand that the genuine homosexual condition, or *inversion*, as it is often termed, is something for which the subject can in no way be held responsible; in itself, it is morally neutral. Like the normal condition of heterosexuality, however, it may find expression in specific sexual acts; and such acts are subject to moral judgement no less than those which may take place between man and woman. It must be made quite clear that the genuine invert is not necessarily given to homosexual practices, and may exercise as careful a control over his or her physical impulses as the heterosexual; on the other hand, those who commit homosexual acts are by no means always genuine inverts. This suggests a rough but serviceable distinction between the invert proper, and those who may be described as perverts. The *pervert*, as the term implies, is not a true homosexual, but a heterosexual who engages in homosexual practices. He may do so casually, from motives of curiosity or in exceptional circumstances; or habitually, as a prostitute or in pursuit of novel sensual experiences; he may alternate between homosexual and heterosexual activities, or he may confine himself to one or the other for long periods. The pattern of "perversion" is thus one of remarkable complexity, from which some have concluded that there exists a third type, the so-called "bisexual"; but this is very doubtful. It seems to be an inference from observations of sexual behaviour, whereas regard must always be had in the first place to personal sexual orientation. An invert can often engage in heterosexual acts (though to some these are abhorrent), just as a heterosexual can act as a pervert; but in each case the condition of the person concerned is unambiguous. Physical sexual conduct can therefore be misleading, and I have commented in several places upon the sexual adaptability and adventurousness of the uninhibited human being. But of the existence of the genuine, inherent invert there can be no possible doubt.

For the purpose of this essay it is unnecessary to consider in any further detail the causes and character of homosexuality; but the distinction between the *condition* of inversion and the behaviour which I have called perversion is indispensable for a correct interpretation of the historical evidence. I must ask the reader's indulgence for the monotonous repetition of the term "homosexual practices" in these pages; only by its use could the distinction between condition and conduct be preserved.

I ought, perhaps, to make it clear that I am entirely responsible for any interpretations and expressions of opinion contained in this study, which should not be regarded as necessarily representing the views, either of the Council for which I lecture, or of my colleagues in the group which compiled the Report, *The Problem of Homosexuality*.

SHERWIN BAILEY

Birmingham,
   October 24th, 1954.

I

SODOM AND GOMORRAH

1. THE SODOM STORY AND ITS SIGNIFICANCE

CONSIDERATION of the Christian attitude to homosexual practices inevitably begins with the story of the destruction of Sodom and Gomorrah, a catastrophe of which Dr George Adam Smith said that its glare burns still, though the ruins it left have entirely disappeared.[1] This story has exercised a powerful influence, directly or indirectly, upon the civil and ecclesiastical attitudes to sexual inversion and the conduct of the male invert, since it has traditionally been taken for granted that the sin for which the cities were reputed to have been overwhelmed was that of indulgence in homosexual practices between men. So strong has been this belief, that the scene of the crowning offence which precipitated the Divine judgement has given a name to the most reprobated of all modes of coitus, as well as to every kind of sexual act deemed to be contrary to nature. But a consistent tradition does not preclude re-examination of the evidence, and it is important first of all to ascertain the precise character of the sin of Sodom. Among the questions which demand investigation are the following: What is the meaning of the incident recorded in Gen. xix. 4–11? Did that incident simply constitute one proof among many of the wickedness of Sodom—was it the cause, or only the occasion, of God's judgement? What ground is there for the persistent belief that the inhabitants of the city were addicted to male homosexual practices, and were punished accordingly?

---

[1] *The Historical Geography of the Holy Land* (London, 1894), p. 505.

It may not prove possible to answer such questions completely, but the attempt should at least afford some guidance as to the proper interpretation of the Sodom story, and its relevance (if any) to the contemporary problem of the homosexual.

The obvious starting-point for an investigation is the text itself. The story is very familiar. When Lot parted from his uncle Abraham, he decided to settle in Sodom, a city represented in the narrative (along with its neighbour Gomorrah) as exceedingly wicked. God resolved to ascertain for himself the truth about their reputation, and for this purpose two angels were sent to visit Sodom, which they reached one evening, having been brought on their way by Abraham, who had interceded for the city. They were met at the gate by Lot, who pressed them to accept his hospitality. Before they retired that night, the house was beset by the inhabitants, who demanded that the visitors be brought out to them in order that they might "know" them. Lot tried to dissuade them from their purpose, and finally offered to produce his daughters, but without avail. The crowd was thwarted in the end by the angels, who smote the people with blindness; the next morning their visitors took Lot and his family out of the city, and God then overthrew it with brimstone and fire from heaven.

The traditional conception of the sin of Sodom is based on an inference from the demand of the Sodomites: 'Bring them [Lot's visitors] out unto us, that we may know them', and arises from the fact that the word here translated "know" (*yādhaʻ*) can mean "engage in coitus". Is that its connotation in this passage?

The verb *yādhaʻ* occurs very frequently in the Old Testament,[1] yet excluding the present text and its undoubted derivative Judg. xix. 22, it is only used ten times (without qualification) to denote coition.[2] In combination with *mishkābh*, which signifies in

---

[1] According to F. Brown, S. R. Driver, and C. A. Briggs, *A Hebrew and English Lexicon of the Old Testament* (Oxford, 1952), 943 times.

[2] Gen. iv. 1, 17, 25; xix. 8; xxiv. 16; xxxviii. 26; Judg. xi. 39; xix. 25; 1 Sam. i. 19; 1 Kings i. 4.

The Sodom Story and its Significance   3

this context the act of lying, *yādha'* occurs in five further places.[1] On the other hand, *shākhabh* (from which *mishkābh* comes) is found some fifty times meaning "lie" in the coital sense. Moreover, while *yādha'* always refers to heterosexual coitus (omitting from consideration for the present the disputed passages, Gen. xix. 5 and Judg. xix. 22), *shākhabh* is used of both homosexual and bestial coitus, in addition to that between man and woman.

Thus it is exceptional to find *yādha'* employed in a coital sense, and Dr Otto Piper is hardly correct in saying that the Old Testament 'usually describes the act of sexual intercourse by the term "to know" '[2]—though he properly draws attention to the significance of this use of *yādha'*, for coitus between man and woman is a unique and very important means to the attainment of personal knowledge. This in itself, however, emphasizes the heterosexual reference of *yādha'* when used coitally, for the very possibility of "knowing" (in this sense) depends upon sexual differentiation and complementation, and not merely upon physical sexual experience as such.

Linguistic considerations alone, therefore, lend support to Dr G. A. Barton's view that 'there is no actual necessity' to interpret "know" in Gen. xix. 5 as equivalent to "have coitus with", and that it may mean no more than "get acquainted with".[3] Why, then, was an apparently reasonable request made in so violent a manner? What was the wickedness which Lot anticipated, and from which he wished to dissuade the Sodomites? Barton's suggestion that it 'may have been no more than to give the strangers a beating' is hardly convincing, though it does not invalidate his rejection of the coital interpretation of "know". Our ignorance of local circumstances and social conditions makes it impossible to do more than guess at the motives underlying the

---

[1] Num. xxxi. 17, 18, 35; Judg. xxi. 11: '. . . every woman that hath lien by man' (lit., '. . . that hath known lying with a male'); Judg. xxi. 12: '. . . young virgins, that had not known man by lying with him' (lit., '. . . known a man by lying with a male').

[2] *The Christian Interpretation of Sex* (London, 1942), p. 52.

[3] Art. "Sodomy" in *Encyclopædia of Religion and Ethics*, vol. xi, p. 672a.

conduct of the Sodomites; but since *yādha'* commonly means "get acquainted with", the demand to "know" the visitors whom Lot had entertained may well have implied some serious breach of the rules of hospitality. There are several considerations which do, in fact, support this view, and suggest a different explanation of the whole story.

It must not be forgotten that Lot's status in Sodom was only that of a *gēr* or sojourner—that is, a resident alien. In return for the toleration and protection of the city to which he attached himself the *gēr* acquired certain obligations, and there were, no doubt, limitations to his civic privileges which would vary from one community to another. Much would depend upon the way in which a man in such a position comported himself. His attitude no less than his conduct could make his life easy or difficult. Lot does not stand out from the pages of Genesis as a person altogether pleasing in character, and the words of the citizens: 'This one fellow came in to sojourn, and he will needs be a judge', may well imply that he had already made himself somewhat unpopular among them. He may even have given them good cause to regard his actions with suspicion. But unpopularity alone does not sufficiently explain the conduct of the Sodomites towards Lot and his guests—conduct for which there must have been real provocation. Is it not possible that Lot, either in ignorance or in defiance of the laws of Sodom, had exceeded the rights of a *gēr* in that city by receiving and entertaining two "foreigners" whose intentions might be hostile,[1] and whose credentials, it seems, had not been examined? This would afford a natural and satisfactory reason for the investment of Lot's house by the citizens, and for their demand: 'Where are the men which came in to thee this night? Bring them out unto us, that we may know them'—that is, take cognizance of them, and enquire into their *bona fides*. Lot's plea—the plea of a good host—is then perfectly intelligible: '. . . do not so wickedly . . . unto these men do nothing'—in other words: 'Since I have, rightly or wrongly,

---

[1] Cf. Josh. ii.

taken these strangers under my roof, do not now flout the
obligation of hospitality by this unseemly demonstration ... take
no action against my guests, for they are yours also'.[1]

Although the coital interpretation of *yādha'* (and, therefore,
the homosexual interpretation of the Sodom story) is so firmly
rooted in Christian tradition, the alternative non-sexual explanation which has been put forward is at least equally consistent with
the text and the spirit of the narrative; while in certain respects
it is more satisfactory—particularly in that it is consonant with the
Old Testament view of the sin of Sodom, which will be discussed
shortly. This proposed re-interpretation in no way affects the
question of the punishment said to have been inflicted upon the
city and its neighbours. We are simply told that Sodom and
Gomorrah were wicked and grievously sinful, but the writer does
not specify their iniquity more exactly, and only on *a priori*
grounds can it be assumed that it was an iniquity solely or pre-
dominantly sexual in character. The lawless commotion before
Lot's door and the boorish display of inhospitality (coupled, no
doubt, with other signs of wickedness which would not escape
their scrutiny) could well have been sufficient to satisfy the angels
that report was true—and judgement followed accordingly. The
story does not in the least demand the assumption that the sin of
Sodom was sexual, let alone homosexual—indeed, there is no
evidence to show that vice of the latter kind was prevalent there.

One further point requires mention. Lot's proposal to bring out
his daughters in order to indulge the crowd has sometimes been

---

[1] Calvin is one of the few commentators who admit a non-coital meaning for
"know", and he seems to have been a little uneasy about the traditional interpretation of the Sodomites' demand. He suggests that it simply means: 'We wish to
know whom you are bringing as guests into our city', and he, too, implies that
Lot may have given offence by admitting unknown persons into Sodom, where
he was only a *gēr*. Thus Calvin supports to some extent the explanation which I
have suggested. But he cannot rid himself of the traditional assumption that,
whatever Gen. xix means, the Sodomites were homosexual practitioners; he thinks
that their 'imperious expostulation' with Lot for daring to entertain unknown
men was only a device to conceal their real and nefarious design! See *Comm. in
Gen.*, ad loc.

interpreted as an offer of heterosexual in lieu of homosexual
satisfaction—an attempt, so to speak, to divert the lusts of the
Sodomites into less inordinate channels. But the weak and callous
conduct of the 'righteous man'[1] (though partly to be extenu-
ated, perhaps, by the rules of oriental hospitality) needs no such
elaborate explanation, and its connexion with the purpose (whatever it was) for which the citizens demanded the production of
his guests is purely imaginary. No doubt the surrender of his
daughters was simply the most tempting bribe·that Lot could
offer on the spur of the moment to appease the hostile crowd;
and the fact that he could contemplate such a desperate course
may well indicate his anxiety at all costs to extricate himself from a situation which he had precipitated (as already
suggested) by action incompatible with his status in Sodom as
a *gēr*.

So far, it has been assumed that the problem of the Sodom
story is a problem only of interpretation, and that the substantial
truth of the narrative is not in question. But this cannot be taken
for granted, and the historicity of the story and its relation to
folklore and legend have an important bearing upon the significance attached to it. In the days when a radical criticism of the Old
Testament found favour, there were not wanting some who
regarded Gen. xix as nothing more than the Hebrew version of a
universal myth, or as an adaptation for ethical reasons of a legend
designed to account for the peculiarly desolate aspect of parts of
the Dead Sea region, with its grotesque rock formations and its
bituminous deposits. Archæological research, however, has
banished such extreme scepticism. It is now sufficiently established
that the five cities of the Plain (which included Sodom and
Gomorrah) were situated in a fertile tract of country which was
submerged, after their destruction, by the constantly rising waters
of the Dead Sea, so that their ruins lie beneath its present broad
extension to the south of the promontory el-Lisan. We do not
know the precise cause of the disaster which overwhelmed the

---

[1] Cf. 2 Pet. ii. 8

cities, but the evidence of the Bible and of ancient writers, interpreted in the light of modern geological and geographical discovery, allows us to envisage what probably took place. 'A great earthquake, perhaps accompanied by lightning, brought utter ruin and a terrible conflagration to Sodom and the other communities in the vicinity. The destructive fire may have been caused by the ignition of gases and of seepages of asphalt emanating from the region, through lightning or the scattering of fires from hearths'.[1] So sudden and complete a devastation of these prosperous cities would create an indelible impression upon the people of that time who, being ignorant of the scientific explanation, would inevitably tend to ascribe the disaster to supernatural agencies. In this way, no doubt, began the theory of a Divine visitation and judgement for sin, which developed into the familiar Sodom story of the Bible.

To the formation of this story another factor probably contributed. Perhaps the most mysterious feature about the tale is its close general correspondence to others of a similar character in the folklore of various peoples. These legends tell how strangers (sometimes divine beings in disguise, like the angels in the Sodom story) visit a city, where they are refused hospitality. Eventually they find lodging, often with people in humble circumstances— Lot, though not poor, was only a *gēr* in Sodom; and they help their hosts to escape before the city and its inhabitants are destroyed. Of such legends, the best known is that of Philemon and Baucis,[2] and others are noted by Driver[3] and Cheyne.[4] Their ethical teaching is obvious, though it is doubtful whether they were intended to be didactic when they first took shape. Nor do

---

[1] J. Penrose Harland, in "Sodom and Gomorrah", *The Biblical Archæologist* (New Haven, Conn., U.S.A.), vol vi, no. 3, p. 48. For full discussion of the archæological evidence, see the articles in vol. v, no. 2, pp. 17–32 and vol. vi, no. 3, pp. 41–54, where full references are given, both to Biblical and ancient sources, and to modern literature.

[2] Ovid, *Metamorph.* viii. 625 ff.

[3] S. R. Driver, *The Book of Genesis* (Westminster Comm.), p. 203, n. 1.

[4] T. K. Cheyne, art. "Sodom and Gomorrah" in *Encyclopædia Biblica,* iv, coll. 4670–4671.

we know whether any of them had their origin in an actual catastrophe, though this is not improbable. Underlying them all, however, there seems to be an unexplained mythological motif, and this may well account for the particular form which the Sodom story itself assumed during the course of transmission prior to being written down. And if the tale of the natural disaster which overthrew the cities of the Plain was gradually moulded by subconscious influences into yet another version of the basic myth which has just been described, then a further point of some significance emerges. In the legends, as in the Yahwist's narrative in Gen. xix, the conduct which brings judgement upon the offending community and leads to its destruction is never sexual, but always wickedness in general, and in particular, inhospitality. This, again, suggests that the association of homosexual practices with the Sodom story is a late and extrinsic feature which, for some reason, has been read into the original account.

Thus our enquiry has already yielded definite and useful results. It is clear that the destruction of Sodom and Gomorrah was an historical event, and that it was due to natural and not supernatural causes. The tradition that a Divine judgement fell upon the cities because of their wickedness may have been nothing more than a superstitious inference from the awful character of the disaster. If it had any foundation in fact, we still know nothing of the nature of the sin for which it was believed that they had been punished; there is no reason to suppose that it was sexual—still less, that it was homosexual. Nor is any such assumption demanded by the Yahwist's version of the story, which can be interpreted satisfactorily, as we have seen, in an entirely non-sexual sense. But having demonstrated that the Sodom story contains no reference to homosexual practices, we are still no nearer an explanation why it is so commonly associated with such practices in the Christian tradition. We must now turn, therefore, to a survey of the sources from which that tradition was derived, in order to locate its origin and trace its growth.

2. THE "HOMOSEXUAL" INTERPRETATION OF THE SIN OF SODOM

In this section we shall examine the evidence of the canonical Scriptures; the Apocrypha, Pseudepigrapha, and other Jewish writings to the end of the first century A.D.; and Rabbinical and Patristic literature; dealing with the material chronologically wherever possible.

The Old Testament depicts Sodom as a symbol of utter destruction,[1] and its sin as one of such magnitude and scandal as to merit exemplary punishment,[2] but nowhere does it identify that sin explicitly with the practice of homosexuality. If the passages in question now suggest the commission of unnatural acts, it is because of the associations which have collected around the name of Sodom. The following citations clearly imply that the city and its neighbour were destroyed because of their general wickedness and corruption:

GEN. xiii. 13: ' . . . the men of Sodom were wicked and sinners before the Lord exceedingly.'

GEN. xviii. 20: '. . . the cry of Sodom and Gomorrah is great . . . their sin is very grievous . . .'

JER. xxiii. 14: 'In the prophets of Jerusalem also I have seen an horrible thing; they commit adultery, and walk in lies, and they strengthen the hands of evil-doers, that none doth return from his wickedness: they are all of them become unto me as Sodom, and the inhabitants thereof as Gomorrah.'

EZ. xvi. 49–50: 'Behold, this was the iniquity of thy sister Sodom; pride, fulness of bread, and prosperous ease . . .; And they were haughty, and committed abomination (*tōʿēbhāh*) before me: therefore I took them away as I saw good.'

The word *tōʿēbhāh*, which appears in the last passage, is sometimes thought to denote "abomination" of a particularly sexual

---

[1] Isa. i. 9; xiii. 19; Jer. xlix. 18; l. 40; Amos iv. 11; Zeph. ii. 9.

[2] Gen. xiii. 13; xviii. 20; Deut. xxix. 23; Jer. xxiii. 14; Lam. iv. 6; Ez. xvi. 50; cf. in the New Testament Matt. x. 15; xi. 23–24; Lk. x. 12; 2 Pet. ii. 6–8; Jude 7; Rev. xi. 8.

kind, and might, therefore, in its context here suggest the commission of homosexual acts. Primarily, however, it refers to idolatry, for which it is a conventional term in the Old Testament; and undoubtedly this is its meaning in Ez. xvi. 50.[1] It has no warrantable homosexual implications, though it is admittedly open to misinterpretation in the light of later presuppositions concerning Sodom. It should be remembered that although the practice of idolatry often involved religious prostitution and other forms of sexual immorality, there is no reason to suppose that these were normally other than heterosexual in the cults with which the Hebrews were familiar at this time.[2]

The witness of the Old Testament is maintained in the Apocrypha, where three passages tell only of the folly, pride, and inhospitality of the Sodomites, and call for no special comment—apart from the fact that the second seems to suggest that the Egyptians surpassed the Sodomites in wickedness:

> WISD. x. 8: '. . . having passed wisdom by, not only were [the inhabitants of the cities] disabled from recognizing the things which are good, but they also left behind them for human life a monument of their folly; to the end that when they went astray they might fail even to be unseen. . . .'

> WISD. xix. 8: '. . . whereas the men of Sodom received not the strangers when they came among them; the Egyptians made slaves of the guests who were their benefactors.'

> ECCLUS. xvi. 8: God 'spared not those with whom Lot sojourned, whom he abhorred for their pride.'

Indeed, it is not until we reach the late New Testament books, 2 Peter and Jude, that we find the sin of Sodom connected in any way with homosexual practices. Since the passages in question, however, show clear evidence of the influence of the Pseudepigrapha, it will be convenient to defer consideration of them for the present. Meanwhile, it is plain that the traditional conception of Sodom receives little support from Scripture.

---

[1] For a further discussion of the meaning of *tō'ēbhāh*, see p. 43.
[2] See also pp. 51 f.

In confirmation of this general conclusion, it is significant that none of the Biblical condemnations of homosexual practices[1] makes any mention of the Sodom story—a remarkable and inexplicable omission, if in fact it was commonly believed that the destruction of the city was a Divine judgement upon the unnatural proclivities of its inhabitants. Only in one place is there the faintest possibility of a suggestion in this direction. In terms of St. Paul's teaching about the 'wrath of God' in Rom. i. 18 ff., the catastrophe which overtook the cities could be regarded as an illustration of cause and effect in the moral realm. But the Apostle does not expressly associate 'that recompense of their error which was due' to homosexual perverts with the fall of Sodom and Gomorrah—and it is all too easy to interpret such a passage in conformity with the assumptions of later times. Augustine, it may be noted, explains homosexual perversion as being itself a "recompense" for other offences, since such unseemly acts are not only sins *per se*, but also the penalties for sins.[2]

We now turn to the Palestinian Pseudepigrapha, where we find a more fruitful field of research. In the *Book of Jubilees,* which depicts an uncompromising Judaism of the most rigid and conservative orthodoxy, there are three passages referring to Sodom. One simply echoes Gen. xiii. 13:

JUB. xiii. 17: '. . . the men of Sodom were sinners exceedingly.'

but the other two introduce a new theme:

JUB. xvi. 5–6: '. . . the Lord executed his judgements on Sodom, and Gomorrah, and Zeboim, and all the region of the Jordan, and he burned them with fire and brimstone, and destroyed them until this day, even as [lo] I have declared unto thee all their works, that they are wicked and sinners exceedingly, and that they defile themselves and commit fornication in their flesh, and work uncleanness on the earth. And in like manner, God will execute judgement on the

---

[1] Lev. xviii. 22; xx. 13; Rom. i. 26–27; 1 Cor. vi. 9–10; 1 Tim. i. 10. There are also certain possible or dubious allusions to homosexual practices, but none of these refer to Sodom.

[2] *de nat. et grat.*, xxii.

places where they have done according to the uncleanness of the Sodomites, like unto the judgement of Sodom.'

JUB. XX. 5–6: 'And [Abraham] told [his sons and grandsons] of the judgement of the giants, and the judgement of the Sodomites, how they had been judged on account of their wickedness, and had died on account of their fornication, and uncleanness, and mutual corruption through fornication.

> "And guard yourselves from all fornication and uncleanness,
> And from all pollution of sin,
>
> Lest ye make our name a curse,
> And your whole life a hissing,
>
> And all your sons to be destroyed by the sword,
> And ye become accursed like Sodom,
> And all your remnant as the sons of Gomorrah." '

Here there is a marked emphasis upon sexual sin, and a corresponding indifference to the arrogance and inhospitality stressed in the Old Testament and the Apocrypha. But the most interesting feature occurs in Jub. xx. 5, where "the judgement of the Sodomites" is associated with "the judgement of the giants". The latter are the "sons of God" mentioned in Gen. vi. 1–4, the "angels" of 2 Pet. ii. 4 and Jude 6, and the Watchers of Jewish legend,[1] who are represented as lusting after mortal women and descending to earth in order to enjoy coitus with them. The consequence of these incongruous unions of the divine and the human is described by our author in a passage which is significant because it repeats the terms "fornication . . . uncleanness" which figure prominently in Jub. xvi. 5 and xx. 5–6:

JUB. vii. 20–21: Noah 'exhorted his sons to . . . guard their souls from fornication and uncleanness and all iniquity. For owing to these three things came the flood upon the earth, namely, owing to the fornication wherein the Watchers against the law of their ordinances went a-whoring after the daughters of men, and took themselves wives of all which they chose: and they made the beginning of uncleanness.'

---

[1] Cf. Enoch vi–x; Jub. vii. 21 f., x. 5 f.; Test. Reub. v. 6–7; Test. Naph. iii. 5.

Obviously both "fornication" and "uncleanness" in this passage relate to the unlawful intercourse, as a result of which (according to Jub. vii. 22) the *Nāphīdim* (i.e., *N^ephīlīm*) or Giants were engendered. The recurrence of these words in Jub. xx. 5, where they are used to describe the sin which provoked both "the judgement of the giants" and "the judgement of Sodom", seems to indicate that the writer intended to draw a parallel between two occasions when illicit sexual conduct called forth the vengeance of the Almighty. From this we would infer that the "uncleanness" of which the Sodomites were guilty corresponded to that of the Watchers in that it was heterosexual, and consisted in the commission of adultery, and of acts of gross sexual licence and shameless promiscuity between men and women. By contravening "the law of their ordinances" in seducing mortal women, the Watchers had "made the beginning of uncleanness"; and their evil example was followed by the Sodomites who were given, not to seduction and rape, but to "mutual corruption through fornication"—each sex deliberately enticing the other to immorality.

Thus the author of the *Book of Jubilees* clearly departs from the general tradition of Scripture both in stressing the sexual character of the sin of Sodom, and in connecting the overthrow of the city with the Watcher story and the Flood; but it does not seem, from the evidence just considered, that he interpreted the Sodom story in a homosexual sense—indeed, his emphasis appears to be wholly heterosexual. It will be well, however, to postpone a final estimate of his views until we have examined a passage from the almost contemporaneous *Testament of Naphtali*, one of the *Testaments of the Twelve Patriarchs* (c. 109–106 B.C.), a Palestinian work of Pharisaic origin. In this passage the Watcher-Flood motif reappears:

> TEST. NAPH. iii. 4–5: '... recognizing ... in all created things, the Lord who made all things, that ye become not as Sodom, which changed the order of nature. In like manner the Watchers also changed the order of their nature, whom the Lord cursed at the flood. ...'

Here, the offence of both Watchers and Sodomites is said to have consisted in changing the "order of nature"—an order which is inherent in the creation because it is God's handiwork, and which can easily be perceived when all things are related to their Author, who designed them to obey his laws and to fulfil his will. In the view of the writer, the Watchers subverted this natural and evident order by their "fornication" and "uncleanness"[1]—that is, by the unlawful mingling in coitus of two incongruous elements, the divine and the human. It is clear how they can be said to have transgressed what the *Book of Jubilees* calls "the law of their ordinances", but it is not equally plain how it was believed that Sodom "changed the order of nature". It can scarcely be doubted, however, that the context implies some kind of sexual sin, and three explanations suggest themselves.

Since the offence committed by the Watchers was unquestionably heterosexual, so too, it may be argued, was that of the Sodomites. If, therefore, the "order of nature" be interpreted to mean the principles of human sexual relation by which it is the will of God that the intercourse of men and women should be governed, then the sin of Sodom is easily explained in terms of any behaviour which contravenes those principles. Fornication, adultery, incest, promiscuous coitus—all can properly be described as changing the "order of nature", since they defeat the essential purpose of sexual union, which is the establishment of a permanent and exclusive *henosis*, or community of man and woman in "one flesh", based on free and responsible choice in love. There is, however, one prohibitive objection to this interpretation. It presupposes a conception of sexual relation more elevated and personalized than any known to have been current in antiquity, either within or outside Judaism; and it is extremely improbable that the author was so far in advance of contemporary thought in regard to marriage—especially since the rest of his work does not

---

[1] These terms occur in 1 Enoch x. 9 and 11, as well as in Jub. xvi. 5 and xx. 5–6; and in Enoch they refer expressly to the unions between the Watchers and the women.

justify any such assumption. Though he would undoubtedly have deplored all heterosexual irregularities, it is unlikely that he would have condemned them as contrary to nature in the sense implied by the text. We must therefore seek elsewhere for its meaning.

It is possible that the phrase, "changed the order of nature", refers to some transgression which was inordinate in itself, and not simply in its circumstances. In this case, interpretation will depend upon whether the sexual significance of the passage is regarded as primary, or only as incidental. Supposing it to be primary, we might well infer that the author intended to attribute to the Sodomites the practice of abnormal modes of coitus; and since bestiality is never imputed to them by ancient writers (though it is sometimes connoted by a loose use of the term "sodomy"), this could only mean that he believed that they were addicted to homosexual acts.

On the other hand, the author's argument at this point suggests that if the text has any sexual significance, it is peripheral rather than central. Having stated that the Sodomites 'changed the order of nature', he goes on to say: '*in like manner* the Watchers also changed the order of their nature', implying that both had committed a similar breach of the universal principle of order established by the Creator. Now we have already seen that the sin of the Watchers, according to the *Book of Jubilees,* was not a sexual sin alone, but that their chief offence consisted in unlawful commerce with an incompatible order of beings—the daughters of men. It is significant, therefore, that human and divine beings also figure in the Yahwistic version of the Sodom story, and that the tradition whose origin we are investigating associates this story with an alleged attempt by the Sodomites to have homosexual coitus with their supernatural visitors. Have we, in Test. Naph. iii. 4, a conception of the sin of Sodom in which the sexual element is subsidiary, and which emphasizes rather the lawless violation of the bounds which separated the angels from men, and confined each order to its appointed realm?

This interpretation is supported by a New Testament passage

in which the influence of these pseudepigraphical texts can be easily detected:

> JUDE 6–7: 'And angels which kept not their own principality, but left their proper habitation, he hath kept in everlasting bonds under darkness unto the judgement of the great day. Even as Sodom and Gomorrah, and the cities about them, having in like manner with these given themselves over to fornication, and gone after strange flesh (*hetera sarx*), are set forth as an example, suffering the punishment of eternal fire.'

Here the sin of Sodom is identified even more explicitly with that of the Watchers, while at the same time greater stress is laid upon its sexual character. Nevertheless, Jude does not ascribe the punishment of the Sodomites to the fact that they purposed to commit homosexual acts *as such*; their offence was rather that they sought to do so with "strange flesh"—that is, with supernatural, non-human beings. In his view, therefore, the sin of Sodom, though admittedly sexual ('having . . . given themselves over to fornication'), was only, as it were, incidentally homosexual; the emphasis is rather upon the sexual incompatibility of the angelic and human orders than upon any particular kind of unnatural coitus between persons of the same sex.

It is interesting to note that in taking over this passage from Jude, the author of 2 Peter makes certain alterations, and introduces the figure of Lot:

> 2 PET. ii. 4, 6–8: 'For if God spared not angels when they sinned, but cast them down to hell, and committed them to pits of darkness, to be reserved unto judgement . . . and turning the cities of Sodom and Gomorrah into ashes condemned them with an overthrow, having made them an example unto those that should live ungodly; and delivered righteous Lot, sore distressed by the lascivious life (*hē en aselgeia anastrophē*) of the wicked (for that righteous man . . . vexed his righteous soul from day to day with their lawless deeds [*anoma erga*]): . . .'

He substitutes for the specific charges of fornication and lusting after "strange flesh" the more general accusations of lasciviousness (*aselgeia*) and lawless deeds. Furthermore, he does not directly connect the sin of the Sodomites with that of the angels, nor does he associate the overthrow of the cities expressly with any particular act of disobedience—though possibly he intended that the reader should draw the obvious inference from the mention of Lot and his deliverance. These changes may indicate a desire to avoid the inconveniences of too close a parallel between the Watcher and the Sodom stories, either because the author favoured the Old Testament view of the sin of Sodom, or because the emphasis upon the incongruity of sexual union between human and divine beings tended to hinder a fully homosexual interpretation of the Sodom story. But whatever may be the explanation of the differences between Jude and 2 Peter here, it is evident that by the end of the first century A.D., though the sin of Sodom is still regarded as a transgression of "order", there is now also a perceptible emphasis upon its homosexual implications.

We can now return to the question of the meaning of Test. Naph. iii. 4–5. Having already rejected a purely heterosexual interpretation, we are thus left with two plausible explanations. The text itself does not markedly favour one more than the other, though there are indications, as we have seen, that the author may well have attached greater importance to the transgression of "order" than to the particular sexual acts which the Sodomites are alleged to have premeditated or committed. But each of these aspects undoubtedly contributed to his notion of the sin of Sodom, and the fact that he seems to have connected the city's trespass with both the practice of homosexuality and an attempt to have unlawful intercourse with celestial beings is particularly suggestive. It affords good reason to suppose that these two ideas had already coalesced to produce a new, but as yet somewhat inchoate conception of the sin of Sodom which differed in certain respects from that of Scriptural tradition, and which had begun to replace the latter in the circles from which the Pseudepigrapha emanated.

If this inference is substantially correct, it enables us to locate the source of the Christian interpretation of the Sodom story, and also to account for the marked similarity of thought and idiom displayed by the passages relating to Sodom in the *Book of Jubilees* and the *Testament of Naphtali*—a similarity which is clearly to be explained by the common theory underlying them. Although neither of these works explicitly associates Sodom with homosexual practices, there is thus a strong presumption in favour of the view that some such connexion, more or less definite, existed in the minds of the authors—though the comparison of the Sodomites with the Watchers seems to have been prompted in the first place chiefly by the transgression of "order" in which both sinned against nature. We may conclude, therefore, that the development which we are attempting to trace began at least as early as the second century B.C., and that its influence is probably to be detected in the *Book of Jubilees,* despite the absence of any explicit allusion to homosexual acts.

In the *Testaments of the Twelve Patriarchs* there are four other references to Sodom, two of which are found in passages belonging to the original version. One of the latter is vague:

> TEST. ASH. vii. I: 'Become not, my children, as Sodom, which sinned against the angels of the Lords, and perished for ever.'

Here the reference may be to the inhospitality of the Sodomites; if any allusion to a sexual sin was intended by the author, there is no indication as to what he had in mind. The other passage is more explicit:

> TEST. BENJ. ix. I: 'And I believe that there will be also evil-doings among you . . .; that ye shall commit fornication with the fornication of Sodom, and shall perish, all save a few, and shall renew [or better, perpetrate[1]] wanton deeds with women . . .'

Even here, however, we are left to guess the precise nature of the "fornication of Sodom". The phrase would admit of a homosexual interpretation and may thus reflect the influence of the new conception of the sin of Sodom which seems to have been

---

[1] See R. H. Charles, *The Testaments of the Twelve Patriarchs* (London, 1908), p. 210 and note ad loc.

winning acceptance at this time; on the other hand, it may simply denote conduct so profligate as to deserve the exemplary punishment meted out to the Sodomites and their neighbours.

It is just possible that the author may have meant this text to be a "prophetic" reference by the Patriarch to the incident related in Judges xix, when the Benjamites acted towards a travelling Levite much as the Sodomites had behaved towards the angels, and also grievously violated his concubine, so that she died. The close affinity between this narrative and Gen. xix would account for the mention of Sodom, while the abuse of the concubine would explain the words: 'ye . . . shall perpetrate wanton deeds with women'. But although the story of the outrage at Gibeah doubtless acquired its traditional (but quite unwarranted[1]) homosexual associations because of its similarity to the Sodom story, we know nothing of any contemporary interpretation which would throw light upon the meaning of "the fornication of Sodom" in this passage, and it must therefore remain an open question whether or not the latter has any reference to homosexual practices.

The two remaining passages occur among some polemical additions which were made to several of the *Testaments* during the period 70–40 B.C.:

> TEST. LEV. xiv. 6: 'And out of covetousness ye shall teach the commandments of the Lord, wedded women shall ye pollute, and the virgins of Jerusalem shall ye defile; and with harlots and adulteresses shall ye be joined, and the daughters of the Gentiles shall ye take to wife, purifying them with an unlawful purification; and your union shall be like unto Sodom and Gomorrah.'

> TEST. NAPH. iv. 1: '. . . I have read in the writing of Enoch that ye yourselves also shall depart from the Lord, walking according to all the lawlessness of the Gentiles, and ye shall do according to all the wickedness of Sodom.'

There is no doubt that Test. Lev. xiv. 6 refers to the mixed marriages which were so much abhorred by the stricter Jews. If

---

[1] See the discussion of this story, pp. 53 f.

the writer had adopted the new homosexual conception of the sin of Sodom, which is not improbable, the text may mean that he regarded such marriages as no less unnatural than the practices attributed to the Sodomites—though the comparison would appear to be somewhat forced. On the other hand, as we shall see, Sodom came also to be associated with barrenness, and it is more likely that this passage simply declares that unions with Gentile women contracted in defiance of the law will be cursed with sterility, so that a man's line will perish as certainly as did the cities of the Plain.

The "writing of Enoch" to which the author of Test. Naph. iv. 1 refers is probably a lost Enochic work written in Hebrew. On portions of this book were based certain passages in *The Book of the Secrets of Enoch,* a Hellenistic Jewish work composed in Egypt before the middle of the first century A.D., which is usually cited as 2 Enoch. Dr Charles regards Test. Naph. iv: 1 as a loose adaptation of the following passage:[1]

> 2 ENOCH xxxiv..2: '[The idolaters] . . . have laden the whole earth with untruths, offences, abominable lecheries, namely one with another, and all manner of other unclean wickednesses, which are disgusting to relate.'[2]

Unless the phrase, "abominable lecheries, namely one with another", is merely tautologous, there would seem to be no doubt that it relates to homosexual practices,[3] thus affording evidence that by approximately 50 B.C. at the latest the interpolators of the *Testaments of the Twelve Patriarchs* regarded the sin of Sodom as involving unnatural vice.

But Test. Naph. iv. 1 is also interesting in that it suggests a close connexion between the "wickedness of Sodom" and "the lawlessness of the Gentiles". This is significant, for it is well known

---

[1] W. R. Morfill and R. H. Charles, *The Book of the Secrets of Enoch* (Oxford, 1896), pp. xxiii–xxiv and 49, note ad loc.

[2] Translation from R. H. Charles, *The Apocrypha and Pseudepigrapha of the Old Testament* (Oxford, 1913), ii, pp. 452–453.

[3] In the translation of 2 Enoch in W. R. Morfill and R. H. Charles, op. cit., the term "sodomy" is actually used in this passage.

that homosexual perversions were common in the Hellenistic world, as indeed 2 Enoch xxxiv. 2 implies. We shall have to consider later the possibility that the origin of the homosexual interpretation of the Sodom story is to be explained by the Jewish reaction to a closer acquaintance with pagan immorality during the three centuries immediately preceding the Christian era.

Another passage, this time from the later stratum of 2 Enoch, clearly identifies the iniquity of the Sodomites with the moral corruption of Hellenistic society in one of its most typical forms:

> 2 ENOCH x. 4: 'This place [the northern region of the third heaven] is prepared for those who dishonour God, who on earth practise sin against nature, which is child-corruption after the Sodomitic fashion, magic-making, enchantments and devilish witchcraft, and who boast of their wicked deeds, stealing, lies, calumnies, envy, rancour, fornication, murder . . .'

It is evident that among the Jews of the Dispersion the conception of the sin of Sodom had undergone considerable change since the author of 3 Maccabees (c. 100 B.C.) wrote:

> 3 MACC. ii. 5: 'Thou didst burn up with fire and brimstone the men of Sodom, workers of arrogance, who had become known of all for their crimes, and didst make them an example to those who should come after.'[1]

Philo, who was roughly contemporaneous with the author of 2 Enoch, expressly associates Sodom with homosexual practices. In one treatise he states that "Sodom" signifies blindness and sterility,[2] and that "know" (*yādha'*—*suggignomai*) in Gen. xix. 5 means "servile, lawless, and unseemly pederasty [lit., 'unseemly and male pederasty']"—this, apparently, being the first instance of the express attribution of a homosexual coital connotation to the word "know" in this text.[3] But the most interesting passage

---

[1] The preceding verse mentions the Watcher story, but without any sexual implication: 'Thou didst destroy those who aforetime did iniquity, among whom were giants trusting in their strength and boldness. . . .'

[2] *Quæst. et Solut. in Gen.* iv. 31.

[3] Ibid., iv. 37.

occurs in the treatise *De Abrahamo*, where Philo allows his imagination full scope in a description of Sodom and its inhabitants which owes nothing to Genesis, however largely it may be indebted to the social underworld of first-century Alexandria:

> DE ABR. xxvi [134–136]: 'The land of the Sodomites . . . was brimful of innumerable iniquities, particularly such as arise from gluttony and lewdness (*lagneia*) . . . The inhabitants owed this extreme licence to the never-failing lavishness of their sources of wealth . . . Incapable of bearing such satiety . . . they threw off from their necks the law of nature, and applied themselves to deep drinking of strong liquor and dainty feeding and forbidden forms of intercourse. Not only in their mad lust for women did they violate the marriages of their neighbours, but also men mounted males without respect for the sex nature which the active partner shares with the passive; and so when they tried to beget children they were discovered to be incapable of any but a sterile seed. Yet the discovery availed them not, so much stronger was the force of the lust which mastered them. Then, as little by little they accustomed those who were by nature men to submit to play the part of women, they saddled them with the formidable curse of a female disease. For not only did they emasculate their bodies by luxury and voluptuousness, but they worked a further degeneration in their souls and, so far as in them lay, were corrupting the whole of mankind.'[1]

Here at last we have the Sodom of nameless and unmentionable vices which has obsessed the minds of the theologian and the legislator for so many centuries; but it is not the Sodom of the Bible, wicked though that city was, by the general consent of the Scriptures. Philo's Sodom is located, not in the submerged vale of Siddim, but on the shores of the Mediterranean, and its life has been depicted in even more lurid detail by Petronius and Juvenal. It is most unlikely, however, that this is a picture of his own invention. Other writings, as we have seen, contain hints in this direction, and Philo was doubtless only expressing in somewhat vivid language a conception of Sodom and its offence which had

---

[1] Transl., F. H. Colson, in the Loeb Classics ed. of Philo's *Works*, vi, pp. 69–71.

gradually established itself among the Jews both of Palestine and of the Dispersion during the preceding two centuries.

In briefer terms Josephus (37/38–c. 96) presents the same view. Describing in his *Antiquities* the overthrow of Sodom, he says:

> ANT. I. xi. 1 [194–195]: 'About this time the Sodomites grew proud, on account of their riches and great wealth: they became unjust towards men, and impious towards God . . ., they hated strangers, and abused themselves with Sodomitical practices. God was therefore much displeased at them, and determined to punish them for their pride. . . .'

Later in the same account, his language betrays the influence of contemporary life:

> ANT. I. xi. 3 [200]: 'Now when the Sodomites saw the young men [the angels] to be of beautiful countenances, and this to an extra-ordinary degree . . . they resolved themselves to enjoy those beautiful boys by force and violence. . . .'

Not all references to Sodom are so explicit, however, even at this period. The *Biblical Antiquities*, a work of about A.D. 70, probably of Palestinian origin and wrongly attributed to Philo, does not mention the visit of the angels or the destruction of the city, and simply notes that 'the men of Sodom were very evil and sinners exceedingly'.[1] The *Testament of Isaac* (c. A.D. 100 ?), a Hebrew work which underwent some alteration by a Christian hand, contains a description of the torments inflicted upon sinners in hell, among whom are certain who are 'plunged down into the cold, these are they that have committed the iniquity[2] of Sodom, and so they are tormented exceedingly'.[3] But there is good ground for the belief that by the end of the first century A.D. the sin of Sodom had become widely identified amongst the Jews with homosexual practices.

It is the more remarkable, therefore, that Rabbinical literature reflects scarcely anything of this development. Only once is

---

[1] viii. 2.   [2] *anomia* in the Greek version.
[3] Transl. by. S. Gaselee in the Appendix to G. H. Box, *The Testament of Abraham* (London, 1927), p. 69.

homosexuality expressly associated with Sodom. In the Midrash on Genesis the demand of the Sodomites to "know" the visitors is interpreted sexually,[1] and in explanation of this it is stated:

> GEN. RABBAH, l. 7: 'The Sodomites made an agreement among themselves that whenever a stranger visited them they should force him to sodomy and rob him of his money.'

Even this, however, does not attribute to the Sodomites the practice of homosexual vice habitually among themselves, but suggests that sodomy was an indignity reserved for strangers, and that this outrage, accompanied by violence and robbery, was the most serious and reprehensible feature of the inhospitality for which they were famed.

The meaning of Gen. xiii. 13: 'Now the men of Sodom were wicked and sinners against the Lord exceedingly', came in for some discussion among the Rabbis. A common interpretation was that the Sodomites were wicked in this world with their bodies, and sinners in the world to come, being excluded therefrom; but the Patriarch Judah preferred to say that they were wicked with their bodies and sinners with their money, because they were mean and uncharitable.[2] The Midrash on Genesis expounds this text thus: the Sodomites were "wicked" to each other, "sinners" in adultery, "against the Lord" in practising idolatry, and "exceedingly", because of the blood which they shed.[3] The Talmud also repeats the familiar charge that they waxed haughty because of the good which God had lavished upon them.[4] Apart from the single allusion in the Midrash to adultery, no sexual (let alone homosexual) implication can be read into these conceptions of the sin of Sodom; the phrase, "wicked with their bodies" seems to mean nothing more than "wicked in their deeds".

Traditionally, the offence of the Sodomites was supposed to be that of the dog-in-the-manger—hence the appellation, a "a man of Sodom", given to anyone who adopted such an attitude.[5]

---

[1] *Gen. Rabbah*, l. 5.   [2] *Bab. Sanhed.* 109a; cf. Mishnah, *Sanhed.* x. 3.
[3] *Gen. Rabbah*, xli. 7.   [4] *Bab. Sanhed.* 109a.
[5] *Bab. Erub.* 49a; *Bab. Keth.* 103a; *Bab. Baba Bath.* 12b, 59a, 168a; *Bab. Aboth* 5 (cf. Mishnah, *Aboth* v. 10).

It is also interesting to note that the names assigned to the legendary judges of Sodom are likewise free from sexual associations. In the Talmud four are mentioned—Liar, Awful Liar, Forger, and Justice-Perverter;[1] and in the Midrash five—False-Principles, Lying-Speech, Cad, Justice-Perverter, and Man-Flayer.[2] Thus there is little in Rabbinical writing to support the opinion that the Sodomites were given to the practice of homosexual vice, save the isolated allegation that they were in the habit of subjecting strangers to the act of sodomy.

The Fathers of the Christian Church, on the other hand, entertained no doubt whatever that the Sodomites were peculiarly and inordinately addicted to homosexual practices, and that they were punished on this account. It would be tedious, however, to present the evidence in full, and four representative passages will suffice to indicate the general view during the Patristic period:[3]

CLEMENT OF ALEXANDRIA, *Paed.* iii. 8: The Sodomites had '. . . through much luxury fallen into uncleanness, practising adultery shamelessly, and burning with insane love for boys.'

JOHN CHRYSOSTOM, *ad pop. Antioch. hom.* xix. 7: '. . . the very nature of the punishment was a pattern of the nature of the sin. Even as [the Sodomites] devised a barren coitus, not having for its end the procreation of children, so did God bring on them such a punishment as made the womb of the land for ever barren and destitute of all fruits.'

AUGUSTINE, *de civ. Dei*, xvi. 30: Sodom, '. . . the impious city, where custom had made sodomy as prevalent as laws have elsewhere made other kinds of wickedness.'

---

[1] *Bab. Sanhed.* 109b.   [2] *Gen. Rabbah*, l. 3.

[3] For other references to the sin of Sodom, see Ephraim the Syrian: *Hymns on the Faith*, i. 26, *Hymns on the Nativity*, i; John Chrysostom: *in Heli. et vid.* iv, *de perf. carit.* vii, *in Matt hom.* xlii. 3, *in epist. ad Rom.* iv, *in epist. I ad Thess.* viii. 3, *in epist. ad Tit. hom.* v. 4; Augustine: *de mend.* vii [10], *contra mend.* ix [20, 22], xvii [34], *Conf.* iii. 15, and cf. *de fid. spe et carit.* lxxx; Gregory: *dial.* iv. 37, *moral.* xiv. 19; *Const. apost.* vi. 27–28; and in the apocryphal literature, *vis. Paul.* xxxix. Usually printed with the works of Tertullian there is an anonymous and somewhat incoherent poem, *Sodoma*, in which the Sodomites are clearly depicted as pæderasts.

CONST. APOST. vii. 2: ' "Thou shalt not corrupt boys": for this
wickedness is contrary to nature, and arose from Sodom . . .'

Despite occasional allusions to its arrogance and inhospitality, and
to the wealth and plenty which were supposed to have led to its
fall,[1] the Sodom of the Old Testament and the Apocrypha clearly
had no place in the thought of the Early Church, but only the
Sodom of Philo and Josephus, in which homosexual vice, and
especially that associated with the "love of boys", was believed
to have been rampant.

Thus the traditional Christian opinion that the Sodomites were
annihilated because of their homosexual practices can be traced to
its origin in a conception of the sin of Sodom which appeared first
in Palestine during the second century B.C. In the beginning this
conception was undeveloped and somewhat confused, and was
not exclusively or even mainly homosexual, for the connexion
between the Sodom story and that of the Watchers in the *Book of
Jubilees* and the *Testaments of the Twelve Patriarchs* suggests that
the offence of the Sodomites was regarded principally as a transgression of "order". But in the additions to the *Testaments,* and
notably in Philo and Josephus, the idea of the sin of Sodom
became at once more clearly defined and more restricted; the
Watcher element fell into the background or disappeared entirely,
and the homosexual aspect remained predominant. It is not
surprising that the Pseudepigrapha should thus have influenced
the Christian interpretation of the Sodom story, for these writings,
some of them highly apocalyptic in character, made a ready
appeal to Christians; on the other hand, they lay right outside
the mainstream of Rabbinical tradition and were never recognized by Judaism, which explains the almost negligible effect of
the new theory upon the Talmud and the Midrash.

None of the sources which we have examined states why a new
version of the sin of Sodom arose to supersede the old, but Test.
Naph. iv. 1, as we have seen, hints at an explanation by associating

---

1 Cf. Justin, *I Apol.* liii; John Chrysostom, *in Matt. hom.* vi. 9, xiii. 2, lvii. 5,
in epist. ad Rom. iv, *in epist. ad Hebr.* xxix. 4; John Cassian, *Instit.* v. 6; also *Acta
Pauli*—§iv in M. R. James, *The Apocryphal New Testament* (Oxford, 1924), p. 284.

"the wickedness of Sodom" with "the lawlessness of the Gentiles". This lawlessness, in the eyes of the Jews, took many forms, but there is no doubt that it was exemplified conspicuously in the debased *paiderastia* and the homosexual perversions which were common in Hellenistic society, and that the pseudepigraphical references to Sodom reflect a revulsion from practices which were more or less tolerated by the easy-going morality of many pagans. In the Hebrew tradition Sodom had become a symbol rather than a locality; in its clamant iniquity it stood for every wickedness which offended the devout Jewish spirit—pride, inhospitality, adultery, forgetfulness of God and ingratitude for his blessings. What was more natural than that the conception of Sodom should change with the times—that it should become the symbol of the peculiar vices of Hellenism, which were abhorrent not only in themselves, but as the depravities of an alien and hostile culture?

Here, undoubtedly, we find the origin of the homosexual interpretation of the sin of Sodom which has so profoundly influenced Christian thought legislation. and So firmly established has it become that its authenticity is accepted without question, not only by theologians and lawyers, but also by specialists such as Ellis[1] and Kinsey,[2] from whom criticism of such a tradition might have been expected; while the acquiescence of the homosexual himself is indicated by his description of homosexual society as the "world of Sodom"[3]! Nevertheless, our investigation shows that there is not the least reason to believe, as a matter either of historical fact or of revealed truth, that the city of Sodom and its neighbours were destroyed because of their homosexual practices. This theory of their fate seems undoubtedly to have originated in a Palestinian Jewish reinterpretation of Gen. xix, inspired by antagonism to the Hellenistic way of life and its exponents, and by contempt for the basest features of Greek sexual immorality.

---

[1] H. Ellis, *Studies in the Psychology of Sex* (Philadelphia, 1918), ii, p. 3.

[2] A. C. Kinsey and others, *Sexual Behaviour in the Human Female* (London, 1953), p. 482, n. 24.

[3] Cf. D. W. Cory, *The Homosexual Outlook* (London, 1953), pp. 99. etc.

From this part of our enquiry, therefore, we may conclude that the Sodom story has no direct bearing whatever upon the problem of homosexuality or the commission of homosexual acts. Hence it is no longer possible to maintain the belief that homosexual practices were once punished by a Divine judgement upon their perpetrators so terrible and conclusive as to preclude any subsequent discussion of the question. Still less can it be held that an act of God has determined once for all what attitude Church and State ought to adopt towards the problem of sexual inversion. This is not to say that homosexual acts may not, in a greater or lesser degree, be sinful; but only that their morality falls to be decided (like that of other human acts) by reference to the natural law, and in accordance with the principles of Christian ethics and moral theology, and cannot be considered settled by a natural catastophe which occurred in the remote past.

II

THE BIBLE AND HOMOSEXUAL PRACTICE

1. DEFINITE REFERENCES

HOMOSEXUAL practices are very rarely mentioned in the Bible, though references to adultery and to heterosexual fornication are numerous. In all, there are only six passages which undoubtedly relate to homosexual acts; five refer to males and one to females, and they condemn such practices in general terms, without any precise specification or distinction. Two passages are to be found in the "Holiness Code" of Leviticus:

LEV. xviii. 22: 'Thou shalt not lie with mankind, as with woman-kind: it is abomination (*tō'ēbhāh*).'

LEV. xx. 13: '. . . if a man lie with mankind, as with womankind, both of them have committed abomination (*tō'ēbhāh*): they shall surely be put to death; their blood shall be upon them.'

These laws cannot be accurately dated, so we do not know whether they reflect an early or a late attitude to homosexual practices; moreover, it is difficult to say whether they were dictated by the exigencies of some particular social situation, or whether they are simply items of abstract legislation designed to provide against a future possible occurrence of the offences penalized. The "Holiness Code" was once regarded as exilic and associated with the school of Ezekiel, but the tendency now is to treat it as pre-exilic, and even to assign it to a time prior to Deuteronomy—that is, to the seventh century B.C. The precise date and provenance of individual laws and prohibitions is even less certain. Those under discussion, for instance, may belong (at least in substance) to a period considerably earlier than the time when the "Holiness Code" was compiled; on the other hand, they may not originally have formed part of the Code, but may have been added by an editor during the process of incorporating it into the Priestly document, or "P"—the latest of the primary sources of the Pentateuch.

Dr S. R. Driver considers that Lev. xviii. 22, and perhaps Lev. xx. 13, may be aimed at the offence condemned in Deut. xxiii. 17,[1] but this is unlikely. It has generally been supposed that the Deuteronomic passage refers to male homosexual temple prostitution, but this surmise is groundless, and due mainly to misunderstanding of the function of the *qādhēsh*—a word unfortunately translated "sodomite" in the Authorized and Revised Versions of the English Bible.[2] It is hardly open to doubt that both the laws in Leviticus relate to ordinary homosexual acts between men, and not to ritual or other acts performed in the name of religion. But we do not know whether such practices were common among the Hebrews, nor does there seem to be any record as to how often, if ever, the death penalty ordered by Lev. xx. 13 was actually enforced.

The fact that these laws occur in chapters which expressly associate homosexual and other immoralities with the customs of the Canaanites and the Egyptians[3] may suggest that the object of this legislation was rather to prevent the contamination of God's people by the depravities of the heathen than to extirpate the vices of Israel. This view, however, presupposes that the nations with which the Hebrews were in contact indulged in homosexual practices to an extent that made their influence dangerous, and the evidence is worth examination, both because of its bearing upon the passages under consideration, and for its general interest in connexion with the subject of this study.

From Egyptian sources we do not gain much assistance. Havelock Ellis states that 'more than four thousand years ago

---

[1] S. R. Driver, *Deuteronomy* (International Critical Commentary series, Edinburgh, 1896), p. 264.

[2] See below, pp. 49 f.   [3] Cf. Lev. xviii. 3 and 24–30; xx. 23.

homosexual practices were so ancient that they were attributed to the gods Horus and Set,'[1] but without further explanation such an assertion is calculated to mislead.[2] The allusion is to an incident in a folk-tale dating from 2000–1900 B.C. which recounts the well-known rivalry between the two gods. Their animosity eventually reached such a pitch that they were summoned to appear before the other gods, who bound them to lay aside their quarrel and to keep the peace. Thereupon Seth professed to be reconciled with Horus, and invited him to pass "a happy day" in his house—a proposal which Horus accepted in good faith, not suspecting that Seth's intentions were less friendly than his words. The story describes the sequel to this visit:

THE CONTENDINGS OF HORUS AND SETH, xi. 3–4: 'And when it was eventide the bed was spread for them, and they twain lay down. And in the night Seth caused his member to become stiff, and he made it go between the loins of Horus.'[3]

Later, Seth demanded the office of Ruler, declaring that he had 'performed doughty deeds of war' against Horus.[4]

This claim suggests a clue to the meaning of the incident. There is evidence that among both Egyptians and other peoples sodomy was regarded as an indignity suitable for infliction upon a defeated enemy—partly, no doubt, because it would add to the humiliation of the conquered by treating them as if they were women. Whether in fact the defeated were ever thus brought into contempt has not been proved, but there is no doubt of the belief that such a custom existed,[5] and the celebration of a victory may

---

[1] *Studies in the Psychology of Sex* (Philadelphia), ii (2nd ed., 1918), p. 9.

[2] Ellis rarely subjected his historical gleanings to critical analysis, but accepted them (often from secondary sources) at face value. Here he gives as the source of his information 'a Fayum papyrus, found by Flinders Petrie, translated by Griffiths (*sic*), and discussed by Oefele'—in a German periodical devoted to dermatology! The translation in question is possibly that of a fragmentary Middle Kingdom papyrus in F. Ll. Griffith, *Hieratic Papyri from Kahun and Gurob*.

[3] Transl. A. H. Gardiner, *The Chester Beatty Papyri*, I (Oxford, 1931), p. 21.

[4] *The Contendings* . . . , xii. 3 ; A. H. Gardiner, op. cit., p. 22.

[5] See A. H. Gardiner, op. cit., p. 22, n. 2

have involved acts of ceremonial pæderasty.[1] Further supporting
evidence is provided by one of a collection of spells belonging to
the Vth or VIth Dynasties, and intended for the benefit of a dead
king:

> UTTERANCE 372 (652a): 'Go forth, plant thyself on him [the
> enemy] that he may not copulate with thee.'[2]

Thus it would appear that the act perpetrated surreptitiously upon
Horus by Seth was really a stratagem by means of which the latter
sought to ensure that he should be regarded as victorious over his
rival—hence his assertion: '. . . as to Horus, this same that
standeth here, I have performed doughty deeds of war against
him'.

Ellis says of the Egyptians, 'it would seem that they never
regarded homosexuality[3] as punishable or even reprehensible',[4]
but the belief that it was customary, or at any rate appropriate, to
humiliate the vanquished by subjecting them to sodomy is proof
in itself that they did not look upon homosexual acts between
men as entirely honourable. There is also the witness of the
"Protestation of Guiltlessness" (1750–c. 1580 B.C.), in which the
dead man confesses before his judges:

> A. 20: 'I have not had sexual relations with a boy.'

> B. 27: 'O His-Face-Behind-Him, who comes forth from *Tep-het-
> djat*, I have not *been perverted*; I have not had sexual relations with
> a boy.'[5]

These asseverations admittedly refer expressly to acts committed
with boys, and there is nothing to indicate whether the practices
of adults were viewed more leniently. But the general impression
left by such meagre evidence as we possess is that the ancient

---

[1] See G. D. Hornblower, "Further Notes on Phallism in Ancient Egypt", in
Man, 1927, vol. xxvii, § 97. 3, p. 151.

[2] Ibid.

[3] In the context, this word undoubtedly means homosexual acts.

[4] Op. cit., p. 9.

[5] Transl. in J. B. Pritchard (ed.) *Ancient Near Eastern Texts relating to the Old
Testament* (Princeton, 1950), p. 34.

Egyptians regarded homosexual practices as in some degree morally objectionable and personally degrading, from which we may conclude that such practices were not so common among them as Leviticus would seem to imply.

The situation in Assyria and Babylonia is as difficult to assess as that in ancient Egypt. According to Ellis, the Code of Hammurabi (c. 1900 B.C. ?) indicates that homosexuality was practised in Assyria,[1] but the extant portions of the Code do not expressly mention the fact, and nothing therein can be construed as implying any reference to it. Dr Kinsey says that the Gilgamesh epic 'contains passages suggesting homosexual relations' between Gilgamesh and Enkidu,[2] but the text does not seem to support this conclusion.

There are, however, two references to homosexual practices in the Middle Assyrian Laws; the tablets on which these are inscribed belong to the time of Tiglath-Pileser I (twelfth century B.C.), but the laws themselves may go back to the fifteenth century:

TABLET A, § 19: 'If a seignior (*arvēlum*[3]) started a rumour against his neighbour (*tappau*) in private, saying, "People have lain repeatedly with him", or he said to him in a brawl in the presence of (other) people, "People have lain repeatedly with you; I will prosecute you", since he is not able to prosecute (him) (and) did not prosecute (him), they shall flog that seignior fifty (times) with staves (and) he shall do the work of the king for one full month; they shall castrate him and he shall also pay one talent of lead.'

TABLET A, § 20: 'If a seignior lay with his neighbour, when they have prosecuted him (and) convicted him, they shall lie with him (and) turn him into a eunuch.'[4]

---

[1] Op. cit., p. 9.

[2] A. C. Kinsey and others, *Sexual Behaviour in the Human Female* (Philadelphia and London, 1953), p. 481, n. 24

[3] See J. B. Pritchard, op. cit., p. 166, n. 39.

[4] Ibid., p. 181; another version of these laws will be found in G. R. Driver and J. C. Miles, *The Assyrian Laws* (Oxford, 1935), p. 391, but there are only minor verbal differences between the two translations.

These laws afford us some impression of the Assyrian attitude to homosexual practices. Participation in homosexual acts, either actively or passively, by a man of seignioral rank was an indictable offence, and prosecution could take place at the instance of a fellow seignior. Conviction of active sodomy entailed the penalty of castration, and it seems that the offender was himself compelled to submit to the act which he had performed on others; this may have been an application of the *lex talionis*, but it is equally probable that the Assyrians sought to degrade the criminal in the same manner as the Egyptians were reputed to humiliate the vanquished. Passive sodomy was evidently regarded as reprehensible no less than criminal, for a false accusation of habitual addiction to this practice was held to be slanderous and actionable, and incurred severe penalties.

It will be observed that these laws are restricted in their application. In the first place, they deal specifically with offences committed against a man's *tappau* or neighbour, and it has been suggested that 'a slanderous charge of unnatural vice and the commission of this offence itself were only regarded as criminal and therefore taken into consideration by the law, when the victim stood in a specially close relationship to the offender, and were not in other cases punishable'.[1] Secondly, both laws relate only to offenders of seignioral rank; but these limitations do not justify the assumption that homosexual practices were allowed or condoned in the case of men belonging to a lower social class, or that only the *tappau* possessed any right of redress when slanderously accused of being a catamite. The apparently narrow scope of these enactments is probably due simply to the fact that their purpose was solely to define the penalties to which seigniors were liable, the punishment applied to less exalted persons being adjusted according to the crime and the social rank of the accused.[2] Thus there is no reason to suppose that the two laws in question

---

[1] G. R. Driver and J. C. Miles, op cit., p. 71.

[2] There are several examples in the Code of Hammurabi of a gradation of penalties according to social status, the humbler injured party being entitled to a smaller compensation.

do not adequately reflect the Assyrian attitude to homosexual practices, though there is nothing to indicate how prevalent such practices were.

More relevant, perhaps, to our enquiry is the situation among the Hittites, whose cultural influence upon the Hebrews is now acknowledged to have been considerable. It has been asserted that pæderasty was recognized and even legally regulated in Hittite society,[1] authority for this view being claimed from a curious and obscure statute in the code of laws found among the ruins of Boghazköy:

> TABLET I ('If a man'), § 36: 'If a slave gives the bride-price to a free youth and takes him to dwell in his household as husband (of his daughter) no one shall surrender him.'[2]

The words in brackets do not occur in the text itself,[3] and several commentators have held that the law deals with the formation of a homosexual "marriage" between a slave and a free youth—no legal provision being necessary for the establishment of such a relationship between free men. Our knowledge of Hittite law and institutions is admittedly far from complete, but it must be confessed that social approval and statutory regulation of such homosexual unions is a condition of affairs so very extraordinary that this interpretation must be regarded as highly improbable. The addition of the bracketed words makes the law intelligible, and Neufeld's explanation is satisfactory—namely, that it refers to the contraction of a form of what the Hittites termed *erēbu-*marriage, which was similar to the Roman marriage *sine manu*.[4] We may safely conclude, therefore, that this enactment

---

[1] J. Pedersen, *Israel* (Oxford, 4 vols., 1926–1940), i. p. 66—cf. p. 552, followed by D. R. Mace, *Hebrew Marriage* (London, 1953), p. 224.

[2] Transl. in E. Neufeld, *The Hittite Laws* (London, 1951), pp. 10–11; for another version, see J. B. Pritchard, op. cit., p. 194: 'If a slave brings the bride-price to the son of a free man and takes him as husband (*of his daughter*), no one shall change his social status.'

[3] See E. Neufeld, op. cit., pp. 10–11.

[4] Op. cit., pp. 151–152, where the question is discussed and authorities are cited.

does not relate in any way to homosexual relationships or practices.

Another Hittite statute is relevant to our subject, but calls for no special comment:

> TABLET II ('If a vine'), § 189: '. . . If a man sins with a son, (it is) an abomination.'[1]

This is one of several provisions in a law dealing with forbidden sexual practices, but there is no further mention of any kind of homosexual act. Thus the Hittite evidence is particularly meagre, and affords no useful information concerning the attitude of this people to homosexual practices, or the prevalence of such practices among them.

It is sometimes asserted that among the peoples with whom the Hebrews came in contact homosexual practices were customary, and that the Egyptians and Assyrians, in common with other ancient nations, acquiesced in them.[2] It has been shown, however, that this view receives no support from the story of Sodom and Gomorrah, and it is clear from the material which has just been examined that substantiation is equally lacking in Egyptian, Assyrian, and Hittite records. Such practices undeniably existed, but we know nothing of the extent to which they were indulged, and arguments from silence are doubly precarious when sources of information are so few and fragmentary. One thing is certain: the positive evidence which we possess, slight though it is, plainly contradicts the opinion that homosexual practices were accepted without question. As we have seen, the Egyptians numbered corruption of boys among the sins which the soul repudiated at its judgement, the Assyrians penalized homosexual acts by statute, and both regarded passive sodomy in particular as derogatory to human dignity—a humiliation meet for defeated enemies or convicted pæderasts. This can hardly be termed acquiescence,

---

[1] For the text, see ibid., p. 54. J. B. Pritchard, op. cit., p. 196, translates as follows: '. . . . if a man violates his son, it is a capital crime.'

[2] Cf. D. Stanley-Jones, *Sexual Inversion and the English Law* (reprinted from *The Medical Press and Circular*, 12th June 1946, vol. ccxv no. 5588), p. 7.

much less approval; and it is the more difficult, therefore, to understand why Leviticus twice associates homosexual acts, along with other offences, with 'the doings of the land of Egypt' and 'the doings of the land of Canaan'.

There is no reason to suppose that unnatural practices were so markedly characteristic of the nations which surrounded Israel that they specially endangered Hebrew morals. Probably the attribution of such practices to the heathen in the Holiness Code (among other sexual and moral offences) is best explained as an example of the rhetorical denigration to which an over-zealous patriot will sometimes descend, while the enactments themselves were doubtless framed as deterrents to the vicious. Our imperfect knowledge of sexual ideas and customs in the civilizations of antiquity prevents further conjecture concerning the social background and the purpose of Lev. xviii. 22 and Lev. xx. 13. We can only judge from these two laws that the Hebrew attitude to homosexual practices differed but little from that of the Egyptians and Assyrians, as revealed by the records which we have examined; and making due allowance for the paucity of the evidence, we may cautiously hazard the opinion that homosexual practices were ordinarily of infrequent occurrence in Israel. This, of course, does not alter the fact that the Biblical text condemns such practices in the strongest terms; but the force of the Levitical legislation for the Christian Church and for contemporary society must be reserved for examination later.

We come now to the New Testament, where three passages refer to homosexual practices between males:

ROM. i. 27: '. . . the men, leaving the natural use of the woman, burned in their lust one toward another, men with men working unseemliness, and receiving in themselves that recompense of their error which was due.'

I COR. vi. 9–10: '. . . Be not deceived: neither fornicators, nor idolaters, nor adulterers, nor effeminate (*malakoi*—Vulg., *molles*), nor abusers of themselves with men (*arsenokoitai*—Vulg., *masculorum concubitores*), nor thieves, nor covetous, nor drunkards, nor revilers, nor extortioners, shall inherit the kingdom of God.'

I TIM. i. 9–10: '. . . law is not made for a righteous man, but for the lawless and unruly . . . for abusers of themselves with men (*arsenokoitai*—Vulg., *masculorum concubitores*). . . .'

These passages undoubtedly relate to the vices which were common in the degenerate pagan society of the time, and have been depicted in the *Satyricon* of Petronius, the "Epigrams" of Martial, and many other writings in which the authors have recorded for posterity the depravities of their age. Naturally enough, the Bible knows nothing of inversion as an inherited trait, or an inherent condition due to psychological or glandular causes, and consequently regards all homosexual practice as evidence of perversion. Hence the phrase in Rom. i. 27: '. . . leaving (*aphentes*) the natural use of the woman . . .', cannot properly be interpreted as a reference only to the practices of heterosexual males who have abandoned themselves to the illicit satisfactions of homosexual coitus—thus appearing to withhold condemnation from the mutual indulgences of genuine inverts, who could hardly be said to *leave* the "natural use of the woman", for which some of them would have an insuperable aversion, and many a strong distaste. St Paul's words can only be understood in the sense which he himself would have attached to them, without introducing distinctions which he did not intend, and which would have been unintelligible to him.

In 1 Cor. vi. 9 the technical words *malakoi* and *arsenokoitai*, which denote respectively those males[1] who engage passively[2] or actively in homosexual acts, pose a problem which translators have not always happily solved. In the Authorized and Revised versions "effeminate" hardly conveys the precise sense of *malakoi* to the modern reader, while "abusers of themselves with mankind", though not inadequate, is somewhat vague in that it could stand as a rendering of either *malakoi* or *arsenokoitai*, and

---

[1] In view of Rom. i. 26 (discussed below), it is curious that St Paul does not mention women who engage in homosexual practices (*tribades* or *hetairistriai*).

[2] In the context, standing as it does between *moichoi* and *arsenokoitai*, there is little doubt concerning the sexual reference of *malakoi* though, like its Vulgate equivalent, *molles*, it could also denote "faint-hearted" or "cowardly".

would be better if it were not preceded by "effeminate". Some
translators have taken refuge in euphemisms or conventional
expressions: the *Twentieth Century New Testament* (1902) is
content with "immoral", which serves as an inclusive term for
moichoi (adulterers), *malakoi,* and *arsenokoitai*; Dr R. F. Weymouth
(1903) has "men guilty of unnatural crime"; and Mgr Knox
(1948) favours "effeminate" and "sinners against nature". Only
Dr Moffatt (1913) offers the simple literal rendering, "catamites
and sodomites".

Although, with the exception of Dr Moffatt's, these translations are in varying degrees inexact or unsatisfactory renderings of
the original, they are otherwise acceptable. But the translation
approved by those responsible for the American Revised Standard
version is unfortunately both inaccurate and objectionable. In
this revision, *malakoi* and *arsenokoitai* are represented by the single
term "homosexuals"; and although a footnote draws attention
to the fact that this expression stands for two Greek words, the
words themselves are not mentioned, their meaning is not
explained, and in particular it is not made clear that they apply
solely to males who engage in homosexual acts. Above all, it is
most regrettable that the revisers should have shown themselves
unaware or unappreciative of the clear distinction which must be
made between the homosexual *condition* (which is morally neutral)
and homosexual *practices.* Use of the word "homosexuals"
inevitably suggests that the genuine invert, even though he be a
man of irreproachable morals, is automatically branded as un-
righteous and excluded from the kingdom of God, just as if he
were the most depraved of sexual perverts. Unless this error is
corrected, and the true meaning of the passage is explained, the
wide circulation of this version and the reputation which its general
merit has won for it may only serve to encourage intolerance and
to perpetuate a great social injustice, thus seriously discrediting
the Christian Church.

In translating 1 Cor. vi. 9 the term "homosexuals" is to be
avoided, for the *malakoi* and the *arsenokoitai* were not necessarily
inverts—indeed, classical literature suggests that many of them

were simply dissolute heterosexuals; while it is a gratuitous libel to imply that the invert is *ipso facto* a *malakos* or an *arsenokoitēs*. Only Dr Moffatt's concise and accurate rendering does justice to St Paul's precision of terminology, and it is to be hoped that his version will ultimately command general approval, unless an equally exact and more acceptable alternative can be found.

The last reference to claim our attention occurs in St Paul's Epistle to the Romans, and it will be convenient to set it in its context, though this will mean repeating a passage which has already been quoted and examined:

> ROM. i. 26–27: '. . . God gave them up unto vile passions: for their women changed the natural use (*phusikē chrēsis*) into that which is against nature: and likewise (*homoiōs*) also the men, leaving the natural use (*phusikē chrēsis*) of the woman, burned in their lust one toward another, men with men working unseemliness. . . .'

Although the phrase, "their women changed the natural use into that which is against nature", appears to relate to homosexual practices between females, it is in fact somewhat ambiguous, and could admit of a heterosexual interpretation. While the men are described as "*leaving* (*aphentes*) the natural use of the woman" and taking to homosexual acts, it is only said of the women that they "*changed* (*metēllaxan*) the natural use . . .", no details of their conduct being given. This might suggest that the Apostle's object was to illustrate the moral corruption of the heathen by showing how their women encouraged heterosexual perversions, while their men went further, and resorted to homosexual practices. In this case, *homoiōs* would imply a general similarity in the behaviour of the sexes in that both had acted unnaturally by giving rein to "vile passions", rather than a specific similarity such as a homosexual interpretation would require. Even so, it is not clear how the women "changed the natural use". Nothing more might be meant than the adoption of variations in coital position or method,[1] though the sexual practice of antiquity included a wide

---

[1] Ovid (*Ars amat.* iii. 777–778) and Apuleius (*Metamorph.* ii. 17), among others, describe the reverse of the supposedly "natural" coital position (i.e., that in which

variety of erotic indulgence which could be regarded as contrary to the "natural use".[1]

On the other hand, *homoiōs* in this passage may signify that in "working unseemliness" with one another the men had done precisely as the women, thus relating the text under discussion directly to tribadism. Of the two interpretations, the second is perhaps on the whole the more probable, though even the first would not exclude a reference to Lesbian as well as to heterosexual practices. Despite the ambiguity, therefore, we may conclude that in Rom. i. 26 it is likely that St Paul was alluding to homosexual acts between females, and that here we have the only mention of such acts in the Bible.

2. POSSIBLE REFERENCES

In the Revelation of St John there are two passages which have often been regarded as bearing upon the subject of this study:

/ REV. xxi. 8: 'But for the fearful, and unbelieving, and abominable (*ebdelugmenoi*), and murderers, and fornicators, and sorcerers, and idolaters, and all liars, their part shall be in the lake that burneth with fire and brimstone; which is the second death.'

/ REV. xxii. 15: 'Without are the dogs (*kunes*), and the sorcerers, and the fornicators, and the murderers, and the idolaters, and every one that loveth and maketh a lie.'

According to Dr H. B. Swete, the *ebdelugmenoi* are those who have practised 'the monstrous and unnatural vices of heathendom',[2] while Dr R. H. Charles says that they are 'those who are

---

the woman lies beneath the man), and it is interesting that Sanchez (*de matr.* iii) regarded the woman's adopting an incumbent position as the "use against nature" of Rom. i. 26. Certain theologians have held that woman's subordination to man requires her to assume a succumbent role—and subordination was a cardinal feature of the Pauline theory of sexual relation (cf. 1 Cor. xi. 3 f.). Thus it is not impossible that Rom. i. 26 refers to the coital variations practised in the first century. Cf. also Lucretius, *de rerum nat.* iv. 1263–1267 (*c. a posteriori*).

[1] Cf. Apuleius, *Metamorph.* iii. 21, and Martial, *Epigr.* ix. 67, for instances of one practice.

[2] H. B. Swete, *The Apocalypse of St John* (London, 1907), p. 282.

defiled with the abominations referred to in [Rev.] xvii. 4–5, connected with the worship of the Beast and generally with the impurities of the pagan cults, including unnatural vice'.[1] Martin Kiddle, however, simply defines "abominable" as 'a general term for all defiled by pagan cults',[2] and Archbishop Carrington appears to take the same view.[3]

Both Swete[4] and Charles[5] identify the *kunes* with the *ebdelug-menoi*; and Charles supports this identification by reference to the Septuagint text of Deut. xxiii. 18, where *kuōn* translates a technical cultic term *kelebh* which he takes (incorrectly[6]) to be equivalent to 'male [homosexual] prostitute'. Kiddle,[7] on the other hand, does not consider that *ebdelugmenoi* and *kunes* are synonymous, and regards the latter as an addition to the list of evil-doers borrowed from Rev. xxi. 8; but he, too, thinks that *kunes* denotes 'those addicted to unnatural vices.' Lightfoot also, in a note on Phil. iii. 2, assumes that in Rev. xxii. 15 *kunes* is applied to 'those whose moral impurity excludes them from the new Jerusalem'[8]—a definition which would certainly include those who indulge in homosexual practices, though it does not actually specify them. Carrington, on the other hand, describes the inclusion of "dogs" as 'an extra piece of symbolism about the City'. Those who 'nourish their souls on that which is filthy and false' are compared by St John to the 'dirty, mangy curs of the jackal type' which infest the oriental town;[9] they are really the idolaters and the followers after supersitition—and it will be remembered that St Paul applies the term *kunes* in a comparable sense to the Judaizers in Phil. iii. 2.[10]

Thus there is a preponderance of opinion among modern commentators (greater in the case of Rev. xxii. 15 than in that of

---

[1] R. H. Charles, *The Revelation of St John* (Int. Crit. Comm., Edinburgh, 1920), ii, p. 216.
[2] M. Kiddle, *The Revelation of St John* (Moffat Comm., London, 1940), p. 422.
[3] P. Carrington, *The Meaning of the Revelation* (London, 1931), p. 330.
[4] Op. cit., p. 308. [5] Op. cit., ii, p. 178.
[6] See below, p. 51. [7] Op. cit., p. 453.
[8] J. B. Lightfoot, *St Paul's Epistle to the Philippians* (London, 1881), p. 143.
[9] Op. cit., p. 352. [10] See J. B. Lightfoot, op. cit., pp. 143–144.

Rev. xxi. 8) that the *ebdelugmenoi* and the *kunes* in these passages are those who have indulged in immoral sexual acts, and particularly in homosexual practices. Since the respective contexts themselves afford no definite clue to the meaning of these two terms, however, we must consider whether such an interpretation is justified by their intrinsic connotation and their Biblical usage, or whether it has simply been read into them.

Ebdelugmenoi is the perfect participle passive of the verb *bdelussomai,* which means "to feel loathing for", or "to make loathsome" or "abominable". In the New Testament this verb (which occurs twice) and its derivatives *bdeluktos* (abominable—occurring once only) and *bdelugma* (abomination—occurring six times) usually relate to the worship of idols, and never imply any reference to homosexual practice. In the Septuagint, *bdelugma* is used with much greater frequency, chiefly to render the Hebrew words *gillūlīm* (idols, or images), *shiqqūç* (an abomination, or detested thing), *sheqeç* (that which is ceremonially unclean, and consequently "abomination"), and *tōʿēbhāh* (abomination), which appears no less than 116 times in the Old Testament.

Although *tōʿēbhāh* eventually acquired a broad ethical meaning, as many passages in Proverbs show, it always refers primarily to idolatry and apostasy. To describe such "abominations" metaphorical sexual imagery is often employed, and phrases like "committing fornication against Yahweh" or "going a-whoring after strange gods" occur frequently in denunciations of Israel's backslidings. On the other hand, immoral sexual conduct itself (including, as we have seen, homosexual acts between males) is also designated *tōʿēbhāh*: but this does not mean that there is anything peculiarly "abominable" in such behaviour; it is placed in the category of "abominations" because it is typical of the idolater, with his lax moral standards and ethical irresponsibility. But sexual immorality, though a characteristic manifestation of the idolatrous spirit, is not the only kind of offence associated with the service of false gods. Such a worship entirely subverts the true order of things, and its consequences are limitless in their extent and effect; hence all ethical offences must ultimately be regarded as *tō'ēbhāh,* so that 'the final meaning of abomination develops the sense of reversing what is natural', and includes 'anything repugnant to the true nature of a person or thing'.[1]

Although from the Biblical standpoint homosexual practices could thus be regarded as "abomination", this is hardly a sufficient warrant for holding that the special distinguishing mark of the *ebdelugmenoi* was their indulgence in such practices. Even Lev. xviii. 22 and xx. 13 denounce homosexual acts as *tō'ēbhāh* (LXX, *bdelugma*) principally on the ground that they are among the reprehensible customs of the nations from which Israel was required to separate itself—though it is difficult to ascertain the truth of this allegation. The dominant note in the concept of "abomination" is always that of idolatry. The *ebdelugmęnoi* of Rev. xxi. 8 are so termed primarily because of their involvement in pagan worship, by which they have been indelibly defiled; and if they have been guilty of sexual immorality, it is because they have indulged in practices associated with an idolatrous way of life—possibly homosexual acts, but no less probably adultery, religious prostitution, fornication of various kinds, and even, perhaps, bestiality.[2] Thus the interpretations of Kiddle and Carrington represent the limit to which the language of Rev. xxi. 8 will allow us to go, if more is not to be read into *ebdelug-menoi* than is legitimately permissible. Homosexual perverts could well be described in Scriptural terminology as "abominable", but there is nothing to show that by *ebdelugmenoi* the author of the Apocalypse intended to denote the *cinædi* of the contemporary sexual underworld. The only possible conclusion is that *ebdelugmenoi* in Rev. xxi. 8 *might* refer to those who had committed homosexual offences; on the other hand, it could equally well have no homosexual significance whatever.

We now come to *kunes*—the "dogs" of Rev. xxii. 15. In classical Greek, *kuōn* as a word of reproach denotes impudence, shamelessness, audacity, or rashness, while among the Hellenistic

---

[1] K. Grayston, art. "Abomination" in *A Theological Word Book of the Bible* (ed. Alan Richardson, London, 1950), p. 12.

[2] For the last, involving a woman, see Apuleius, *Metamorph.* x. 19 ff.

Jews it was commonly employed to designate the Gentiles, and involved the idea of ceremonial impurity. Although this latter usage is certainly reflected in the New Testament,[1] it can hardly be said to govern the interpretation of *kunes* in Rev. xxii. 15, for the meaning of this term, and of the whole verse, is controlled by the formula: "every one that loveth and maketh a lie": the "dogs", therefore, are really neither Jews nor Gentiles as such, but all who have been corrupted by falsehood, who oppose the Gospel, and who show themselves insensitive to the grace of God.[2] Though they are under the sway of him who is 'a liar, and the father thereof'[3] they are not necessarily guilty of any sexual offence; and there is no warrant for identifying them with the *kunes* mentioned in the Septuagint text of Deut. xxiii. 18, whose duties as temple servants may sometimes have involved acts of heterosexual coitus.[4]

If it is doubtful whether or not *ebdelugmenoi* refers to those who have been guilty of homosexual practices, it will be evident that there is far greater uncertainty concerning the sexual significance (if any) of *kunes*. Therefore, despite the fact that commentators of weight have expressed themselves in favour of a homosexual interpretation in both cases, we can only conclude that it is, at most, possible in Rev. xxi. 8, and extremely improbable in Rev. xxii. 15—and that Carrington's exposition is in each instance the most satisfactory.

3. Homosexual Significance Imputed by Marginal References

In the Wisdom of Solomon there is a passage (xiv. 22 ff.) which describes the scandals and moral evils which result from idolatry, including *geneseōs enallagē*—a phrase which appears to have

---

[1] Cf. Matt. vii. 6 and Phil. iii. 2; also the use of the diminutive *kunarion* in Matt. xv. 26–27 and Mark vii. 27–28.

[2] See Otto Michel, art. *kuōn*, in Kittel's *Theologisches Wörterbuch z. N.T.*, ii, p. 1103.

[3] Jn. viii. 44.   [4] See pp. 51 f.

caused the translators some difficulty, as the following versions show:

> WISD. xiv. 26: '. . . changing of kind . . .' (A.V.).
> '. . . changing of sex . . .' (A.V. marg.).
> '. . . confusion of sex . . .' (R.V.).
> '. . . confusion of kind . . .' (R.V. marg.).

Marginal references in both versions relate this phrase to Rom. i. 26–27, and so, by implication, to homosexual practices; but the selection of these references appears to have been governed entirely by *a priori* considerations, for the precise significance of *geneseōs enallagē* is difficult, if not impossible, to determine.

In classical Greek, *genesis* denotes origin, source, or productive cause; and from these root meanings others are derived—race or descent, production, generation, creation, kind or species, family, and "nativity" in the astrological sense. But neither its primary nor any derived connotation was ever extended to include "sex"; the term *paidoporos genesis* (that through which the child passes at birth) is found as a synonym for the female *genitalia*, but this rare usage gives us no guidance in the present instance. In the Septuagint, *genesis* translates various Hebrew words— *dōr* (age, period, generation), *mishpāchāh* (kind, clan, species), *mōledheth* (kindred, offspring, birth), and *tōlēdhōth* (generations); it stands also for the verb *yāladh* (to be born, to beget), from which the last two terms are derived. In the New Testament, *genesis* only occurs infrequently, and its meaning there and in the papyri conforms to classical usage. Thus the linguistic evidence supports the rendering of *genesis* by "kind", but appears to afford no ground for "sex", which the Revisers preferred.

The other word, *enallagē,* is a derivative of the verb *allassein* (to alter, change, or exchange), and means variation, change, or interchange. In the Septuagint it is found only in the passage under discussion, and is absent from the New Testament and the papyri.

Interpreting the words in their plain sense, it is not easy to extract any satisfactory meaning from *geneseōs enallagē*, particularly when due regard is paid to its context. Of the Scriptural translations, the Authorized Version's "changing of kind" is the most literal, though its significance is far from clear. If, however, "changing of race" were substituted, the passage could well refer to the virtual abandonment of Jewish nationality by Hellenizers who had apostasized to the idolatry of the Greeks—for to cut oneself off from the worship of God was tantamount to severing oneself from God's people.

On the other hand, the Authorized Version marginal reading, "changing of sex", while not strictly accurate, may nevertheless represent an intuition on the part of the translators as to the author's meaning. Supposing this to be the case, *geneseōs enallagē* could be read as an allusion to the wearing of garments belonging to the other sex—a practice denounced and forbidden in Deut. xxii. 5, which extends the prohibition, in the case of a woman, to any article used or carried by a man; those who do such things are *tō'ēbhāh* in the sight of Yahweh. Simulated changes of sex were a feature of many fertility cults, for the assumption of female attire was thought to confer female power upon the wearer, thus enhancing the effectiveness of the reproduction magic performed by the god, or by a priest on his behalf.[1] There is no doubt that the Deuteronomic passage refers to customs connected with the Canaanite and Syrian religions,[2] and *geneseōs enallagē* could equally relate to the rites of the Greek cults and the Mysteries.[3] It could also apply, not to changes of dress, but to the self-castration associated in particular with the worship of Cybele,[4] by means of which the priest or votary imitated the example of Atys, and perhaps at the same time believed that he was assimilating himself to the goddess.

If, however, we follow the Revised Version, and translate *enallagē* by "confusion" (a rendering, it must be admitted, which

---

[1] See L. G. Farnell, *The Cults of the Greek States* (Oxford, 1896 ff.), v., pp. 160–161.

[2] See S. R. Driver, op. cit., p. 250.

[3] Cf. Plutarch, *Quœst. Grœc.* 55, 58; *de mul. virtut.* iv; Joh. Lydus, *de mens.* iv. 46; Lucian, *Calumniœ non temere credendum*, 16; Macrobius, *Sat.* III. vii. 2; Apuleius, *Metamorph.* viii. 24 ff.; Philo, *de spec. leg*, iii. 40; etc.

[4] Catullus, lxiii; Eusebius, *Vita Const.* iii. 55; Augustine, *de civ. Dei*, vii. 26, etc.

appears to extend the sense of the original unwarrantably), several plausible interpretations are possible. The marginal alternative, "confusion of kind", could refer simply to the general effect of Hellenization in obliterating the distinction between Jew and Gentile. More precisely, it could denote either mixed marriages or the *confusio prolis* liable to result from the "disorder in marriage, adultery and wantonness" mentioned in the succeeding phrase. The text reading itself, "confusion of sex", though even more speculative than the marginal variant, could be taken to describe the cultic transvestism or self-mutilation already mentioned; on the other hand it could, of course, be interpreted as an allusion to homosexual practices, while again, it could mean nothing more than effeminacy of manners.

Though all these suggestions are in varying degrees possible, none is entirely satisfactory, and none overcomes the difficulties inherent in the text itself. It can only be said with any confidence that whatever the author intended *geneseōs enallagē* to mean, there seems no reason to suppose that it has any special reference to homosexual acts; the interpretation implied by the marginal note must, therefore, be regarded as arbitrary and without adequate foundation.

4. Homosexual Interpretation Suggested by the Language of the English Version

There are six passages in the Bible, the language of which has been regarded as suggesting a homosexual interpretation. One, the only instance in the New Testament, is too vague to require more than passing notice:

> EPH. v. 12: '. . . the things which are done by them in secret it is a shame even to speak of.'

H. Northcote sees here an allusion to homosexual practices, which are condemned even when they take place 'in circumstances where public decency is not, presumably, infringed'.[1]

---

[1] H. Northcote *Christianity and Sex Problems* (Philadelphia, 1916), p. 289.

Certainly these words, like similar general statements, could apply to the commission of homosexual acts, but on the other hand no such reference may be intended. We do not know what secret and shameful things the author had in mind, though they probably included sexual offences of some sort[1]—and the literature of antiquity supplies evidence enough of the state of contemporary morals. None of the standard commentators is as explicit as Northcote in expounding this passage, and we can only conclude that whatever it may be held to imply, it has no obvious reference to homosexual practice.

In the Old Testament there are five passages, all linked by a common theme, the language of which appears to imply a reference to homosexual practices:

DEUT. xxiii. 17–18: 'There shall be no harlot [A.V., "whore"; A.V. marg., "sodomitess"] of the daughters of Israel, neither shall there be a sodomite (*qādhēsh*) of the sons of Israel. Thou shalt not bring the hire of a whore, or the wages of a dog (*kelebh*), into the house of the Lord thy God for any vow: for even both these are an abomination (*tō'ēbhāh*) unto the Lord thy God.'

✓ I KINGS xiv. 22–24: 'And Judah did that which was evil in the sight of the Lord. . . .For they also built them high places, and pillars, and Asherim, on every high hill, and under every green tree; and there were also sodomites (*qādhēsh* [collective]) in the land: they did according to all the abominations (*tō'ēbhōth*) of the nations which the Lord drave out before the children of Israel.'

✓ I KINGS xv. 12: Asa '. . . put away the sodomites (*qedhēshīm*) out of the land, and removed all the idols that his fathers had made.'

I KINGS xxii. 46: '. . . the remnant of the sodomites (*qādhēsh* [collective]), which remained in the days of his father Asa, [Jehoshaphat] put away out of the land.'

✓ 2 KINGS xxiii. 7: In his efforts to stamp out idolatry, Josiah '. . . brake down the houses of the sodomites (*qedhēshīm*), that were in the house of the Lord. . . .'

---

[1] Cf. Eph. v. 3–5.

Since the term "sodomite" now generally signifies a man who indulges, actively or passively, in homosexual practices, and particularly in anal coitus, these passages are commonly thought to record the condemnation of such persons and their behaviour by Mosaic law and the acts of the righteous kings of Judah. This interpretation is favoured both by commentators and by non-theological writers—such as Westermarck, who assumes that the *qᵉdhēshīm* were male homosexual temple prostitutes, and that sodomy committed with one of them may have been regarded as conferring some supernatural benefit.[1] This view, however, is undoubtedly due to misunderstanding of the function of *qᵉdhēshīm* attached to a fertility cult, for although they had certain religious duties, some of which were probably sexual in character, there is no reason whatever to suppose that they were required or accustomed to perform or submit to sodomy or any other homosexual act for sacred purposes.

It is possible that the Vulgate has partly been responsible for the use of the term "sodomite" in the English versions. In Deut. xxiii. 17 *qādhēsh* is translated *scortator,* which simply means "fornicator", and has no special homosexual significance. But in the other passages *effeminatus* is employed, and this word often serves as a synonym for *pathicus,* which denotes the male homosexual prostitute—one who plays the passive role in sodomy by permitting anal intromission, thus simulating the part of the woman in coitus. "Sodomite" is an appropriate rendering for *effeminatus* (though not for *scortator*), but it does not express the sense of the Hebrew, or the Greek of the Septuagint. In the latter, no less than five different words are used to translate *qādhēsh*: Deut. xxiii. 17 has *porneuōn,* the present participle of *porneuō* (to prostitute, to give oneself to prostitution); I Kings xiv. 24, *sundesmos* (conjunction, connexion)—a word which ordinarily has no sexual significance, but which here means

---

[1] See E. Westermarck, *The Origin and Development of the Moral Ideas* (London, 1908), ii, p. 488; *Early Beliefs and their Social Influence* (London, 1932), pp. 128–129; *Christianity and Morals* (London, 1939), pp. 369–370; also A. C. Kinsey and others, op. cit., p. 482, n. 25; etc.

"coitus" (' . . . there was coitus [not more exactly specified] in the land . . .'); 1 Kings xv. 12, *teletē* (an initiate—? or *hierodoulos*); and 2 Kings xxiii. 7, *kadēseim*—a simple transliteration of the Hebrew. None of these terms suggests any particular reference to homosexual practice. Concerning the remaining passage, 1 Kings xxii. 46, there is some uncertainty, as the Septuagint text is wanting in Codex Vaticanus; it is contained, however, in Codex Alexandrinus, where the collective noun *qādhēsh* is rendered by yet another Greek word, *endiēllagmenos*. This, like *enallagē* (discussed in the preceding section), is a derivative of *allassō* (to alter, change, or exchange), being the perfect participle middle or passive of *endiallassō*, meaning "to alter". It confronts us again with some of the difficulties which we encountered in attempting to determine the significance of *enallagē*; thus the *endiēllagmenos* may be either one who has altered his nature by becoming a homosexual pervert, or one who has been transformed by apostasy from a worshipper of Yahweh into a servant of idols. The correct sense of this word must remain a matter of conjecture, but it seems in any case to be an inaccurate rendering of the original. This brings us to an examination of the meaning of *qādhēsh,* translated "sodomite" in the passages under discussion.

The *qādhēsh,* or "consecrated one", was a male *hierodoulos* or temple servant, and his female counterpart was the *qᵉdhēshāh*—the "harlot", "whore", or "sodomitess" mentioned in Deut. xxiii. 17-18. As these terms suggest, it was normally one of the duties of the *qᵉdhēshāh* to act as a religious prostitute, and her earnings in this capacity were paid into the treasury of the temple she served; probably some *qᵉdhēshōth* also engaged in ritual coitus or other sexual acts when these were required by the cult, but most of them, no doubt, had other functions of a non-sexual nature to discharge in connexion with the temple. Was the ministry of the *qādhēsh* exactly comparable to that of the "sacred woman" in that it involved not only temple service in general, but also some form of prostitution?

It might at first seem that this was not the case, for while *qādhēsh* and *qᵉdhēshāh* are mentioned together in Deut. xxiii. 17, the following verse refers to 'the hire of a whore (literally, "the hire of committing fornication [*zānāh*]")', and 'the wages of a dog (*kelebh*)'—not, as might have been expected, 'the wages of a *qādhēsh*'. This might suggest a second category of male temple servant, whose earnings from prostitution or divination went to enrich the shrine; but another and more likely possibility is that *qādhēsh* and *kelebh* denote different functions rather than different classes of person. From the fact that the term *kelābhīm* ("dogs") appears in a list of the servants and ministers attached to a temple of Ashtoreth in Cyprus,[1] it has been assumed that this was a recognized Phœnician designation for the *qedhēshīm*; but the identification is too uncertain to permit the inference that *qādhēsh* and *kelebh* are always synonymous and interchangeable. Rather, it would appear that *kelebh* signified a *qādhēsh* in the discharge of his function as a procurer of revenue for the temple where he ministered—possibly by exercising gifts of prophecy, and almost certainly by acts of religious prostitution. We may conclude, therefore, that 'the wages of a *kelebh*' to which Deut. xxiii. 18 alludes in conjunction with 'the hire of a whore' were most probably the earnings of a *qādhēsh* in the capacity of sacred prostitute.

It may be doubted whether all *qedhēshīm* acted as *kelābhīm*—but what was the nature of the service rendered by those who did? We may suppose that they served the female devotee in precisely the same way as the *qedhēshōth* served the male, and that their offices were specially in demand by women afflicted with barrenness, who would seek to procure the removal of their reproach by resorting to coitus with a "holy man". Furthermore, *qedhēshīm* probably had ritual sexual functions to perform, whether or not they ministered in the capacity of *kelābhīm*—as, for example, by acting the part of Tammuz to the Ishtar of the *qedhēshōth* in ceremonies designed to promote the fertility of nature by means of homœopathic magic.[2]

---

[1] *Corp. Inscr. Semit.*, I. i. 86; see S. R. Driver, op. cit., p. 264; G. A. Barton, art. "Hierodouloi" in Hastings' *Encycl. of Religion and Ethics*, vi, p. 674b.

[2] See J. G. Frazer, *The Golden Bough, IV: Adonis, Attis, Osiris* (London, 2 vols., 1914–1919), i, pp. 17, 59, 78. Frazer suggests (ibid., p. 76) that the heterosexual

There is no reason to suppose, however, that the *qᵉdhēshīm* were accustomed to indulge in sodomitical acts, or that as *kᵉlābhīm* they engaged in homosexual religious prostitution. Homosexual coitus would be meaningless in the ritual of a fertility cult, with its exclusively heterosexual rationale, and there is no positive evidence that it was ever practised in this connexion. Nor would there be any need for male devotees to seek supernatural benefits from such intercourse, when the *qᵉdhēshōth* were at hand to minister to them. Consequently "sodomite" must be rejected as an inaccurate and misleading translation of *qādhēsh*;[1] it is clear that the passages in which this term appears, far from condemning homosexual practices, have nothing whatever to do with them, and are therefore irrelevant to any discussion of the subject.

5. THE OUTRAGE AT GIBEAH

The story of the outrage at Gibeah, related in Judges xix, affords another instance of a narrative upon which (as upon the Sodom story) tradition has imposed a homosexual interpretation based on *a priori* considerations. There can be little doubt that this story contains a core of truth—that an incident at Gibeah, which may well have involved some sexual offence, led to an attack upon the Benjamites, and to some extent sullied their reputation. But the text as we now have it is the result of a process of recension during which (as even a casual perusal of the narrative will show) the Gibeah story was extensively and, it seems, deliberately assimilated to the Sodom story. Other Scriptural references to Gibeah have led commentators to suppose, with some reason, that the original account may have been adapted for the purpose of

---

functions of the *qādhēsh* may be indicated by the conduct of the sons of Eli (cf. I Sam. ii. 22), but the passage in question ('. . . they lay with the women that did service at the door of the tent of meeting') does not appear in the LXX text of Codex Vaticanus, but in that of Codex Alexandrinus, and is regarded as a late interpolation (see H. P. Smith, *The Books of Samuel* [Int. Crit. Comm.], Edinburgh, 1899, p. 20).

[1] Dr Moffatt's rendering, "catamite", is equally incorrect.

anti-Saul polemic, and in the version now extant there are considerable textual difficulties.[1]

The story itself, as far as it is relevant to this enquiry, can be told in a few words, and its close affinity to Genesis xix will immediately be evident. A Levite, travelling from Beth-lehem-judah to the hill country of Ephraim with his concubine, arrived in Gibeah, a Benjamite city, at night-fall, and was hospitably received by an old man who was a sojourner (*gēr*) there. During the night the Gibeathites beset the house with the demand: 'Bring forth the man that came into thine house, that we may know him.' The host tried to dissuade them from molesting his guest, and offered them his daughter and the concubine instead; at first they refused this bribe, but when the Levite produced the concubine and surrendered her to their pleasure, they took her and 'abused her all the night until the morning', with the result that she died from the effects of their ill-usage. The sequel to this outrage was a punitive campaign in which the other tribes of Israel inflicted a severe retribution upon the Benjamites.

As in the case of the Sodom story, the view that the Gibeathites were prone to homosexual practices and desired the Levite for the satisfaction of their unnatural lusts is nothing more than an inference from the words: 'Bring forth the man . . . that we may know him'[2]—the verb *yādha'* (to know) being again construed in a coital sense. The arguments against such an interpretation have already been reviewed,[3] and the objections noted in connexion with the Sodom story have no less force in the present instance; but there is one further point to consider.

The Gibeathites' demand to "know" the Levite is denounced by his host as wickedness[4] and "folly" (*nebhālāh*); and since *nebhālāh* often relates to sexual offences,[5] and denotes insensibility

---

[1] For a discussion of the textual problems, and of the story generally, see G. F. Moore, *Judges* (Int. Crit. Comm., Edinburgh, 1895), pp. 408–421.

[2] Judg. xix. 22.   [3] See above, pp. 2–3.

[4] '. . . do not so wickedly': the verb is *ra'a'*, which occurs also in Lot's plea in Gen. xix. 7.

[5] Cf. Gen. xxxiv. 7; Deut. xxii, 21: Judg. xx. 6, 10; 2 Sam. xiii. 12—and possibly also Jer. xxix. 23.

to the claims of religion and morality,[1] it has been held that its use here implies that *yādha'* has a coital significance. On the other hand, there is little doubt that the allusion to *n'bhālāh* is an editorial addition made in the process of bringing the Gibeah story into conformity with the Sodom story, and its sexual significance cannot be assumed with certainty. *N'bhālāh* can also denote contumely, disgrace, profanity, and inhospitable churlishness[2]—and the last is a connotation of particular interest in the present context. Presumably the disposition of commentators to attach a sexual interpretation to *n'bhālāh* in Judg. xix. 23–24 has been at least partly due to *a priori* assumptions based upon the parallel Sodom story, for the reference to "folly" need be nothing more than a rhetorical addition designed to emphasize the deplorable lack of courtesy shown by the Gibeathites towards the visitor.

Having regard to the uncertain meaning of *n'bhālāh* and the textual corruption of Judges xix—and above all, to the fact that the narrative in its extant form has obviously been edited so as to make it correspond as far as possible to the Sodom story, we may conclude that there is no reason to suspect the Gibeathites of homosexual proclivities, and that the account of the outrage which they perpetrated has no importance as evidence of the Biblical attitude to homosexual practices. It is interesting to note that Josephus, who has no doubt whatever that the Sodomites desired the angels for sexual purposes,[3] makes no reference to homosexual acts when telling what happened at Gibeah. He says that certain young men, having admired the beauty of the Levite's concubine (who is described as his wife), demanded that she be brought out to them, and when this was refused, took her by force to their own house, where they abused her in the manner described.[4]

---

[1] See the note on *n'bhālāh* in S. R. Driver, op. cit., p. 256.

[2] Cf. especially 1 Sam. xxv. 25.

[3] See above, p. 23. It is, incidentally, a curious feature of the Gibeah story that despite its close correspondence to the Sodom story, there is nowhere in Judg. xix any reference, direct or indirect, to Sodom and the judgment visited upon it.

[4] *Ant.* V. ii. 8 [143–149]. Cf. also the non-homosexual account given in Pseudo-Philo, *Biblical Antiquities,* xlv. 1–4 (ed. M. R. James, London, 1917, p. 204),

6. DAVID AND JONATHAN

The definite Biblical references to homosexual acts are all, as we
have seen, condemnatory, but it is often supposed, nevertheless,
that in the description of the relationship between David and
Jonathan there is at least a tacit approval of homosexual love
between men. We must be clear as to what is meant by this
suggestion. Any relationship between two persons of the same
sex is, strictly speaking, a homosexual relationship, and an
affectionate regard entertained by a man for another man, or a
woman for another woman, is likewise homosexual. But those
who attach a homosexual significance to the intimate friendship
between David and Jonathan either imply (against all the facts)
that both were inverts (which the Old Testament belies by
representing them plainly as normal heterosexual men who
married—David polygynously—and had children), or insinuate
that they gave their "love" physical expression in coital acts, of
which there is no evidence whatsoever. Against all such unfounded
surmises it must be insisted, as Ellis says, that 'there is nothing to
show that such a relationship was sexual'[1] in the colloquial sense
of the word.

The homosexual interpretation of the friendship between
David and Jonathan (that is to say, the suggestion that their
relationship was one which might now be regarded as morally
dubious) rests upon a very precarious basis. No special significance
can be attached to the oriental vehemence with which both men
expressed their emotions when they parted company after Saul had
suspected a conspiracy between them,[2] excessive though it may
seem by comparison with the reticence which our conventions
impose upon male intercourse. Nor must the words of David's
lament be misconstrued; 'Thy love to me was wonderful, passing
the love of women'[3] requires no homosexual interpretation.

---

where there is, however, an allusion to the destruction of Sodom for its wickedness, the nature of which is not specified.

[1] Op. cit., ii, p. 10.
[2] 1 Sam. xx. 41.   [3] 2 Sam. i. 26.

It is simply an acknowledgement of a friendship of remarkable warmth and constancy, such as in those times and under the conditions of martial life and political intrigue would be more likely to subsist between men than between a man and a woman. No one had received better proof than David of the meaning of the "love of women," for not only had his own wife Michal braved the displeasure of Saul her father in falling in love with him, but by a bold subterfuge she had even saved his life.[1] Yet when David was banished, she was given by Saul to Paltiel,[2] and seems to have been reluctant to return;[3] while David himself in exile showed no fidelity to Michal. We can better appreciate his tribute to Jonathan's loyalty and disinterested affection when we take into account the comparatively low conception of marriage which then obtained, and which probably made the "love of women" something hardly to be compared with the "love" of such a comrade as David found in the king's son.

7. Summary of Biblical Evidence

In a recent book about homosexuality the author stated that 'no culture had been more severe in its condemnation than the Hebrews—despite their early approval of homosexuality. About six to seven centuries before Christ, a campaign against the homosexual practices was undertaken, on the grounds that they belonged to a foreign people'.[4] These assertions, which were not documented, are typical of the inaccurate generalizations made by certain writers when dealing with Biblical or ecclesiastical attitudes to sexual matters. There is, in fact, no evidence whatever that the Hebrews had at some time early in their history approved of homosexual practices, while the reference to a "campaign" instituted against such practices is a gross and tendentious exaggeration. If this allusion is to the legislation in Deuteronomy and to the reforms directed against the q^{e}dhēshīm by Asa, Jehoshaphat, and Josiah, then it is irrelevant, since the q^{e}dhēshīm were not

---

[1] 1 Sam. xix. 11–17. [2] 1 Sam. xxv. 44.
[3] 2 Sam. iii. 15–16. [4] D. W. Cory, op. cit., p. 17.

homosexual temple prostitutes. If, on the other hand, the two prohibitions in Leviticus are meant, then to describe these brief items of legislation as a "campaign" is ludicrous, when we do not know in what circumstances or even precisely at what date they were enacted, and have no record of any measures taken to enforce them. Equally unfounded is the statement made by J. Addington Symonds that the laws in question penalized male homosexual acts 'in the interests of population'[1]—an argument which the Bible never advances against such acts.

The attitude of the Hebrews to homosexual practices, as reflected in the Old Testament, was certainly not one of approval or even toleration; yet they do not appear to have regarded sodomy with the same vindictive horror as, for example, the Zoroastrians, for whom it was the worst of all offences against morality.[2] Homosexual acts between females were ignored by the law, but when committed by males such acts, in common with other major crimes,[3] were punished by death—though there is no record (as there is in the case of other capital offences) that the supreme penalty was ever inflicted. It is not even clear precisely what kinds of homosexual act incurred the capital sentence, for the laws term the offence in question not simply lying with a male (which would adequately describe certain forms of homosexual practice), but specifically lying with a male "as with womankind" (*mīshkᵉbhēy'ishshāh*—literally, with "the lyings of a woman": the Septuagint has *koitēn gunaikos* [in Lev. xviii. 22, *koitēn gunaikeian*], and the Vulgate, *coitu femineo*). This qualification may mean that the intention was to penalize only such homosexual acts as approximated to normal heterosexual coitus in so far as they involved penile intromission, and that either no

---

[1] *A Problem in Modern Ethics* (London [privately printed], 1896), p. 6.

[2] M. N. Dhalla, art. "Crimes and Punishments (Parsi)", in Hastings' *Encycl. of Religion and Ethics*, iv. p. 296a.

[3] Among the crimes punishable by death were murder, kidnapping, insult or injury to parents, incest, adultery, certain kinds of fornication, various ritual and religious sins, infant-sacrifice, bearing false witness on a capital charge, and keeping a dangerous ox, if it killed anyone—for refs., see W. H. Bennett, art. "Crimes and Punishments (Hebrew)" in Hastings, op. cit., iv., p. 281.

cognizance was taken of other acts, or they were dealt with as pollutions[1] and were punished less severely. On the other hand, *mīshk^{e}bhēy 'īshshāh* may signify any lying with a male by another male for sexual purposes, such intercourse being only permissible heterosexually. Probably the latter is the more likely interpretation, but it is not certain; and the alternative suggested should not be overlooked when considering the application of the Mosaic laws to modern problems.

The impression we receive from the Bible is that homosexual acts were perhaps relatively uncommon in Israel, but that at least some, if not all, were considered as deeds which merited the severest penalty. In addition, they are included in a catalogue of sexual and other offences which are collectively attributed to the Egyptians and the Canaanites, and are denounced as *tō‘ēbhāh* or "abomination". Research fails to establish any satisfactory positive support for the allegation that homosexual practices were customary among the nations surrounding the Hebrews; rather, the meagre evidence suggests that such practices were variously regarded as criminal, sinful, or personally degrading. It is not impossible, therefore, that the attribution in question is simply a piece of rhetorical denigration—or at most, a polemical exaggeration of heathen vice—designed to intensify Israel's sense of national "holiness" or separation as a peculiar people dedicated to Yahweh. Supposing this to be the case, it would seem that the significance of *tō‘ēbhāh* in Lev. xviii. 22 and xx. 13 has often been misunderstood. This term, as we have seen, is closely associated with idolatry, and designates not only false gods but also the worship and conduct of those who serve them. By a natural extension of meaning, however, it can also denote whatever reverses the proper order of things, and this seems to be the connotation of *tō‘ēbhāh* as applied to homosexual acts in Leviticus. Such acts are regarded as "abomination" not, as Westermarck[2] and others have held, because they were practised by Egyptian or

---

[1] Cf. Lev. xv. 16, etc.

[2] See *Early Beliefs and their Social Influence*, p. 129; *Christianity and Morals*, p. 369; *The Origin and Development of the Moral Ideas*, ii, p. 486.

Canaanite idolaters (for of this there is no proof), but because, as a
reversal of what is sexually natural, they exemplify the spirit of
idolatry which is itself the fundamental subversion of true order.
It is misleading, therefore, to represent the two laws in question
as specimens of Hebrew xenophobia or religious intolerance, or
to accept them, without further corroboration, as an accurate
indication of contemporary pagan morals. They condemn homosexual acts between males (or perhaps only sodomy) as typical
expressions of the ethos of heathenism which Israel must renounce
no less than religious and cultural syncretism with the nations
which bow down to idols.

The attitude of the New Testament to homosexual acts is
determined by the same ethical considerations. St Paul, in the
Epistle to the Romans, expressly denounces both male and female
practices as contrary to nature and characteristic of the "reprobate
mind" of those who, knowing God according to their light, have
nevertheless turned away from truth to falsehood and from
worship of the Creator to the service of idols. The legal penalties
prescribed under the Jewish theocracy can no longer be enforced
by the New Israel, but it is recognized that it falls within the
province of the secular law to restrain and punish (among other
offenders) the *arsenokoitēs* or active homosexual sodomist, while
both he and the *malakos* or catamite are threatened with spiritual
retribution by disinheritance from the kingdom of God—and,
if the *ebdelugmenoi* or "abominable" of Rev. xxi. 8 are homosexual perverts (which is possible, but doubtful), with extinction
at the "second death". Unlike the regulations in Leviticus, which
it is difficult to relate to any concrete social situation or moral
crisis, these New Testament passages show vividly the Christian
reaction to the dissolute sexual behaviour of the Hellenistic world,
which was regarded as the inevitable concomitant of idolatry. In
any final assessment, the development of this attitude cannot be
considered apart from the process of reinterpretation by which
the Sodom story acquired its homosexual significance, with the
consequence that the fate of the city came to symbolize the
retribution awaiting both those who indulge in the vice which is

supposed to have caused its downfall, and the society which condones such depravity of conduct.

The Law, as we have seen, condemned male homosexual practices (or at least sodomy), and punished them with death; the method of execution was not indicated, but the Mishnah and the Talmud prescribe stoning,[1] which from early times was the formal legal mode of carrying out the capital sentence. No cognizance was taken by the law of similar acts between females, and the Talmud regards lesbianism as a mere obscenity; apparently the only penalty incurred was that of disqualification from marriage with a priest in the case of women who practised lewdness with one another.[2]

Various problems of morals and casuistry connected with homosexual practices were discussed by the Rabbis. Thus it was held that the law prohibiting one who had admitted a crime from acting as a witness[3] did not apply where pæderasty had been committed with a man against his will, and that he might therefore combine with another witness to procure the execution of the offender; whereas if the man in question had consented, his evidence must be regarded as inadmissible.[4] It is not stated whether in such cases the man who disclosed his complicity in homosexual acts also incurred the capital sentence equally with his partner, or whether his confession, leading perhaps to the latter's conviction, exempted him from the extreme penalty imposed by Lev. xx. 13 upon both persons concerned. Again, the Mishnah distinguishes between wanton homosexual transgressions, which merited the death sentence, and those which were inadvertent and rendered the offender liable only to a sin-offering; while if it was doubtful whether or not the trespass had in fact occurred, it is laid down

---

[1] Mishnah, *San.* vii. 4; *Bab. San.* 54a.   [2] *Bab. Shab.* 65a.
[3] Cf. Ex. xxiii. 1.   [4] *Bab. Yeb.* 25a.

that a suspensive guilt-offering is incurred.[1] In the case of homosexual acts, as of other forbidden connexions, committed upon one asleep, or upon a minor by one of full age, neither the sleeper nor the minor was regarded as culpable.[2]

The last question is discussed further in the Talmud. In expounding Lev. xx. 13 ('... if a man lie with mankind ...'), it was held that the term "man" excluded a minor—that is, one under the age of thirteen, but that "mankind" signified any male, without distinction of age. This law, therefore, was interpreted as prohibiting an adult male from committing homosexual acts. Furthermore, the Rabbis seem generally to have been of the opinion that the prohibition extended only to active sodomy, and that passive sodomy was forbidden by another law—Deut. xxiii. 17 ('There shall be no ... *qādhēsh* of the sons of Israel'), the correct meaning of which appears by this time to have been forgotten even in learned Jewish circles. According to R. Abbahu, however, R. Ishmael held that the passive sodomist actually incurred penalties under both laws, while R. Akiba, on the other hand, considered that Lev. xx. 13 prohibited both active and passive sodomy—which indeed seems obvious from the wording of the passage in question. The Patriarch Judah maintained that only one capable of active sodomy could, by assuming the passive role, throw guilt upon an active accomplice, but R. Samuel dissented from this view. Opinion varied as to whether or not an active sodomist who was a minor (under thirteen years of age) incurred guilt; Judah held that no guilt was incurred if the passive partner was under nine years of age (that being regarded as the nubile age in the case of a boy), but R. Samuel set the limit as low as three years.[3]

One curious case mentioned in the Talmud is that of homosexual acts involving a *terefah*, or person suffering from an incurable organic disease. It might be thought, said the Patriarch Judah, that no penalty should be incurred for pæderasty with

---

[1] Mishnah, *Kerith.* i. 2.
[2] Mishnah, *Kerith.* ii. 6
[3] For the full discussion, see *Bab. San.* 54a–54b.

such a man, since it is equivalent to abusing one dead. On the other hand, acts from which forbidden pleasure is derived are punishable—and sodomy is such an act; hence Judah concluded that if a *terefah* indulged passively, the active partner was liable to punishment, but if a *terefah* himself took the active role, he was only liable to a penalty if the act occurred in the presence of the Beth Din, or High Court.[1]

Briefly, it may be said that the Jewish Halakah exonerates from the penalty of the law against male homosexual practices only the passive minor, and the active minor if the passive partner is under the age of nine—or three, according to the more severe view. All others committing male homosexual acts actively or passively incur the sentence of death imposed by Lev. xx. 13, which is to be carried out by stoning. As already noted, there is no evidence that this punishment was ever actually inflicted, and the discussions in the Mishnah and the Talmud concerning the application of this law are doubtless mainly theoretical in character. Its severity, however, stands in strong contrast to the lenient view which was taken of female homosexual practices by the Rabbis—and which has, indeed, obtained almost universally. Into this phenomenon we shall have to enquire further in due course.

---

[1] *Bab. San.* 78a.

III

ROMAN LAW TO THE TIME OF JUSTINIAN

1. Pre-Constantinian Legislation and Practice

The Roman law, particularly through the codifications of Theodosius and of Justinian, has exercised a very strong influence, not only upon western European systems of civil and criminal jurisprudence, but also upon the ecclesiastical canon law. It is important, therefore, to ascertain its attitude to homosexual practice.

Originally, it seems that if homosexual practices were ever punished, it was either by private action taken against the offender,[1] or by public process initiated by the ædiles. One celebrated case, probably in the year 226 B.C., was dealt with by accusation before the Senate. It arose from proposals which had been made to the son of the famous M. Claudius Marcellus by C. Scantinius Capitolinus, whom Valerius Maximus describes as tribune of the plebs, and Plutarch as co-ædile with Marcellus. Capitolinus was convicted, and a heavy fine was imposed which Marcellus applied to the purchase of sacred vessels for the temples.[2] As a result of this case the *Lex Scantinia* is supposed to have been passed, by which male homosexual practices were penalized, but in fact the greatest obscurity surrounds both the origin and the provisions of this law, and it is not clear how, if at all, it was connected with the prosecution of Capitolinus. It would have been contrary to Roman usage to name a law after a notorious defendant rather than after its proposer, but it has been suggested that

---

[1] Valerius Maximus, *Memor.* VI. i. 5.
[2] Ibid., VI. i. 7; Plutarch, *Marcell.* ii.

Scantinius himself brought this *lex* forward after his case had ended, in order to vindicate the honour of the *gens Scantinia*. This explanation, though plausible, is hardly convincing, and the Scantinian statute must remain something of a mystery; when invoked, it seems to have been for political rather than moral reasons, and nothing definite is known of any convictions secured under it.

In the year 50 B.C. Pola Servius accused M. Cælius Rufus under the *Lex Scantinia,* and Cælius retorted with a countercharge under the same law against the instigator of the accusation, Appius Claudius Pulcher. Clearly the motive in this case was political, but the outcome is not known—it can hardly have been serious.[1] Undoubtedly political considerations also explain the actions taken under the same law by Domitian (81-96) against certain senators and gentlemen of Rome.[2] Juvenal expresses a desire to see the statute revived,[3] which may indicate that by his time it had either fallen into desuetude or had been repealed; and subsequent references by Ausonius († 393-394)[4] and Prudentius († after 413)[5] do not make it clear whether the law was then in force, or whether the allusions are to an enactment already obsolete.[6] Quintilian († c. 118) mentions the imposition of a fine of 10,000 sesterces for committing homosexual offences, but gives neither the case in question nor the law under which the fine was made;[7] some have assumed that this was the penalty exacted by the Scantinian statute, but this can be nothing more than an unfounded conjecture.

So much for the shadowy *Lex Scantinia,* and the few and meagre allusions to it which occur in Roman history and Latin

---

[1] See Cicero, *Epist. ad Fam.* VIII. xii. 3 and xiv. 4.
[2] Suetonius, *in Domit.* viii.
[3] *Sat.* ii. 43-44.   [4] *Epigr.* xcii.
[5] *Peristeph.* x. 204.
[6] Tertullian also refers to the *Lex Scantinia, de monog.* (c. 217), xii. An allusion supposedly made by Cicero (*Phil.* iii. 6) appears to have been suggested by mis-interpreting "Atinian laws" as "Scatinian laws"; *Scatinia* is sometimes found as a variant spelling of *Scantinia*.
[7] *Inst. Orat.* IV. ii. 69; cf. 71.

literature. There is no further positive evidence concerning homosexual practices and their punishment during the time of the Republic. In 184 B.C. Lucius Quintius Flaminius was ejected from the Senate by Cato for various crimes, among which, it is sometimes inferred, was that of sodomy. There seems little doubt that Quintius had become addicted to unnatural practices during his eastern campaigns and administration, and that his disgrace was precipitated by a murder committed to please a boy to whom he was attached; but it is clear that it was his crime, and not his relationship with the boy or his sexual morals as such, which brought about his downfall.[1] Again, Polybius († *c.* 122 B.C.) asserts that in the Roman army punishment was inflicted upon young men who "abused their bodies" (*parachrēsamenoi tō sōmati*). It has generally been assumed, not without reason, that this refers to indulgence in homosexual acts, but we cannot be certain that Polybius had such practices in mind. The verb *parachraomi* means "to misuse" or "to abuse", and could be applied to auto-erotic or even non-sexual conduct. The nature of the punishment is not stated, and there appears to be no corroboration of this disciplinary measure from any other source.[2]

Although the literature of the time abounds in allusions to homosexual practices, no further mention of legal measures against them is found until the beginning of the third century A.D. When the emperor Severus Alexander († 235) came to power it seems that male homosexual prostitution flourished, regardless of the Scantinian or any other law; indeed, the author of the life of Elagabalus says that pæderasty was "lawful" before the time of the emperor Philip († 249)—though this can hardly mean more than the toleration of *exsoleti,* or mercenary catamites. A tax was actually levied upon them, and upon female prostitutes and procurers, and this formed a useful source of revenue. Alexander diverted the income derived from this taxation so that instead of flowing into the public treasury it went into the fund for restoring the theatre, the Circus, the Amphitheatre, and the Stadium; and it

---

[1] See Plutarch, *Cato,* xvii, and *Flamin.* xviii.   [2] *Hist.* VI. xxxvii. 9.

is said that he contemplated the suppression of the *exsoleti*, but was deterred from his purpose by the fear than an evil recognized by the state (and profitable to it!) might be converted into a vice practised in secret.[1] Not long after, however, Philip took the step from which Alexander shrank, and abolished the prostitution of the *exsoleti*.[2]

These events do little to clarify the position. The fact that the *exsoleti* were tolerated until the time of Philip may mean either that the Scantinian law was no longer in force, or that it was a dead letter, or that its provisions were of no avail in the case of homosexual prostitution—being directed, perhaps, against assault, or designed to protect minors. Consequently when Sextus Empiricus, an early third-century writer, states that among the Romans homosexual practices are forbidden by law,[3] several different interpretations can be placed upon his words. He may mean that the *Lex Scantinia* lay dormant but unrepealed, and capable of being invoked at any time. He may simply allude to the fact that Philip had declared homosexual prostitution illegal. But it is also possible that he had in mind certain opinions and decisions of the great jurists of his day, which appear to extend by interpretation the force of the well-known *Lex Julia de adulteriis coercendis,* so as to make it apply to homosexual offences.

Roman legal theory permitted an extension of the scope of a law in this way. In republican times the opinions of learned lawyers —their interpretations and applications of statute law, and particularly the Twelve Tables—played an important part in the development of Roman jurisprudence; usage gave force to many of these decisions, and they were collected together for reference. Augustus gave formal authority to such opinions by enacting that the answers of the jurists should be solicited and announced, and promulgated under imperial sanction; and Hadrian decided that the rulings of eminent counsel should have the force of law,

---

[1] *Script. Hist. Aug.: Alex.* xxiv. 3–4; cf. xxxix. 2.

[2] *Script. Hist. Aug.: Alex.,* loc. cit.; Aurelius Victor, *de Cæs.* xxviii. 6; cf. *Script. Hist. Aug.: Elagab.* xxxii. 6.

[3] *Hypot.* i. 152.

provided all the respondents concurred. Thus there gradually came into being a corpus of juridical literature which was accepted as having legal authority; to this were added imperial edicts and rescripts, and the whole was finally systematized in the work of the great jurists and scientific commentators.

Unfortunately it is impossible to trace in any precise detail the operation of this interpretative process in the case of the *Lex Julia* (c. 17 B.C.), for its provisions are not fully or exactly known. It is said, however, that among the offences named therein was *stuprum*, the significance of which does not appear to have been clearly defined. According to Papinian († 213) it denotes a sexual offence committed against a virgin or a widow, in contrast to adultery, which involves a married woman.[1] With this definition Herennius Modestinus concurs in one place,[2] but in another he extends the meaning of *stuprum* so as to include sexual acts committed with boys.[3] A contemporary of Papinian and Modestinus, Julius Paulus, states that *stuprum* or any other *flagitium* involving a boy under the age of seventeen (*puer prætextatus*) is a crime meriting capital punishment[4] if the offence was *perfectus*, and banishment to an island if it was *imperfectus*.[5] The distinction here seems to be between acts which were definitely performed and completed, and acts which were only attempted; it is interesting to note that the second of the two penalties recalls that to which an adulteress was liable.[6] Thus there is evidence to suggest that the jurists of the third century were enlarging the scope of the *Lex Julia de adulteriis* by their interpretative commentary, so as to make it applicable also to male homosexual practices—principally, it would seem, with the object of affording

[1] *Dig.* XLVIII. v. 6. § 1.

[2] *Dig.* L. xvi. 101.

[3] *Dig.* XLVIII. v. 34. § 1.

[4] The phrase is *puniuntur capite:* a capital punishment was one affecting the *caput* of a person by depriving him of life, liberty, or citizenship. It is not certain what penalty was intended here, and we cannot assume automatically that it was death; possibly the sentence was left to the discretion of the court.

[5] *Sent.* V. iv. 14 = *Dig.* XLVII. xi. 1. § 2.

[6] Cf. Paulus, *Sent.* II xxvi. 14.

legal protection to minors. Further proof of this development may perhaps be indicated by Marcianus who, in his annotations upon Papinian's treatise *De Adulteriis*, advances the opinion that the penalty for adultery also extends to anyone who, among other offences, lends his house for the purpose of committing *stuprum cum masculo*.[1] It is not clear, however, whether this too is aimed against the violation of boys, or whether it is intended to apply to those who let their premises for the purposes of the *exsoleti*.

During the next three centuries these decisions of the great legists appear to have been accepted without question as constituting a legitimate extension of the original provisions of the Julian law. As a result, either of further interpretative comment, or of the imperial legislation of 390 to which reference will be made shortly,[2] this law seems eventually to have been regarded as covering homosexual offences committed between adults as well as with boys, and its range in the sixth century is sufficiently illustrated by the ninth book of Justinian's *Codex*, tit. ix, *ad legem Juliam de adulteriis et stupro*. This development undoubtedly explains the statement made by Tribonian and his collaborators in the *Institutes* which they compiled at the emperor's bidding, and which was given legal force on 30th December 533:

> INST. IV. xviii. 4: In criminal cases public prosecutions take place under various statutes, including the *Lex Julia de adulteriis*, '. . . which punishes with death (*gladio*), not only those who violate the marriages of others,[3] but those also who dare to commit acts of vile lust with [other] men (*qui cum masculis nefandam libidinem exercere audent*).'

Thus not only are homosexual acts of all kinds regarded as coming within the scope of the Julian law, but now, as *nefanda libido*, every

---

[1] *Dig.* XLVIII. v. 8.

[2] *Cod. Theod.* IX. vii. 6; see pp. 71–72.

[3] According to Paulus, the *Lex Julia* only punished those guilty of adultery with confiscation of part of their property and with relegation to an island (*Sent.* II. xxvi. 14)—a penalty comparable to that inflicted in the case of seduction of a virgin, or a widow of honest character, assuming that no violence was used (see *Inst.* IV. xviii. 4). The death sentence for adultery was introduced, apparently, by Constantine (cf. *Cod. Justin.* IX. ix. 30)—but the authenticity of this law has been questioned.

such act is distinguished from *stuprum,* which a succeeding clause restores to its old meaning as defined by Papinian.

2. The Christian Emperors

Describing the Roman attitude to homosexual practices, Westermarck says that the Scantinian Law 'had lain dormant for ages, and the subject had never afterwards attracted the attention of the pagan legislators. But when Christianity became the religion of the Roman Empire, a veritable crusade was opened against it'.[1] The interpretations of the third-century jurisconsults sufficiently refute the first part of this statement, and show that homosexual practices were by no means indulgently ignored by the criminal lawyers of Rome, especially when minors were concerned. We must now examine the evidence for the "veritable crusade" which the Christian emperors are alleged to have launched.

On 16th December 342 Constantius[2] and Constans promulgated a law, of which the following is a recent translation:[3]

> COD. THEOD. IX. vii. 3 (= COD. JUSTIN. IX. ix. 31): 'When a man "marries" in the manner of a woman, a "woman" about to renounce men, what does he wish, when sex has lost its significance; when the crime is one which it is not profitable to know; when Venus is changed into another form; when love is sought and not found? We order the statutes to arise, the laws to be armed with an avenging sword, that those infamous persons who are now, or who hereafter may be, guilty may be subjected to exquisite punishment.'

Unfortunately this rendering obscures the sense of the opening words: *Quum vir nubit in feminam viris porrecturam,*[4] for *porrigo* does not ordinarily mean "renounce",[5] and there is no reason to suppose that it has any peculiar significance here; a better translation is: "When a man 'marries', [and is] about to offer

---

[1] *Christianity and Morals,* pp. 371–372.
[2] Often confused with Constantine here, e.g., by Ellis, op. cit., ii, p. 346 and by J. A. Symonds, op. cit., p. 8.
[3] By Clyde Pharr, *The Theodosian Code* (Princeton, 1952), pp. 231–232.
[4] See *Corpus Juris Civilis,* ed. Kriegel (Leipzig, 1887), ii, ad loc.
[5] See C. T. Lewis and C. Short, *A Latin Dictionary* (Oxford), s.v.

[himself] to men in a womanly fashion . . ." The commentators
observe that *nubo*, in this context, denotes the part played by the
passive sodomist, as indeed the text itself implies. No reference is
intended to homosexual "marriages", though formal unions of
some kind between men are mentioned by Juvenal[1] and Martial,[2]
and were occasionally celebrated in a spirit of licentious levity, as
in the case of the "nuptials" of Nero and Pythagoras.[3]

It is difficult to know how seriously to take this edict, and
W. G. Holmes remarks that its curious phraseology 'almost
suggests that it was enacted in a spirit of mocking complacency'.[4]
Whether or not this was so, the reference to "statutes" and
"laws" (unless it is merely rhetorical or facetious) would appear
to confirm the conclusion already put forward, that prior to the
accession of Constantine homosexual practices were illegal—
for there is no trace of any legislation against them during the two
decades previous to the issue of this edict. Furthermore, it will be
observed that while the dicta of the jurists in this connexion relate
to the punishment of *stupratores puerorum* or corrupters of boys—
that is, to active pæderasts, the law of Constantius and Constans
appears to be directed against passive sodomists and may, if conceived in a serious vein, be aimed at the suppression of prostitution
by *exsoleti*. If so, it is apparent that Philip's reform was short-lived.

Nearly fifty years after the enactment of this statute, another
law was put forth by Valentinian II, Theodosius, and Arcadius on
6th August 390. This is particularly notable because it prescribes
the penalty of burning, which was (theoretically) the commonest
criminal punishment imposed upon sodomists during the Middle
Ages, and persisted (at least nominally) in some countries until
recent times:[5]

COD. THEOD. IX. vii. 6: 'All persons who have the shameful
custom of condemning a man's body, acting the part of a woman's,

[1] *Sat.* ii. 117 ff.   [2] "Epigrams", xii. 42.
[3] See Tacitus, *Ann.* xv. 37, etc.
[4] *The Age of Justinian and Theodora* (London, 2 vols., 1912), i. p. 121.
[5] See E. Westermarck, *Christianity and Morals*, p. 372 and n. 6; H. Ellis, op.
cit., ii, p. 347.

to the sufferance of an alien sex (for they appear not to be different
from women), shall expiate a crime of this kind in avenging flames
in the sight of the people.'[1]

Whatever dubiety there may be concerning the previous law,
there can be none about the temper of this, though its meaning is
nevertheless somewhat uncertain. If it is interpreted strictly
according to the letter, it would appear to be aimed either at the
active sodomist (thus reinforcing the decisions of the jurists, and
supplementing the provisions of the former statute, which
penalizes the catamite), or at those who procure men or boys for
the purpose of prostitution. On the other hand, the wording is
such that it could be construed as relating to any homosexual act—
that is to say, the "shameful custom of condemning a man's
body . . . to the sufferance of an alien sex" could be held to
include the practice of the catamite in submitting his own body
for abuse. On the whole the literal interpretation seems preferable,
in the absence of any definite indication as to the intentions of the
legislators; we may regard this law, therefore, as directed against
active sodomy and, perhaps, against organized homosexual
prostitution.

It is evident, however, that the latter continued to flourish, and
that this vice of the Old Rome found its roots also in the New, for
we learn of its existence in Constantinople at the beginning of the
sixth century from the historian Evagrius, who describes how the
emperor Anastasius I abolished a tax called the *chrusarguron*. This,
he explains, was imposed upon certain small wage earners, upon
whores who plied their business in low and obscure brothels, and
'upon those who were devoted to a prostitution which outraged
not only nature but the common weal'[2]—the last, without doubt,
being *exsoleti*. Evagrius indignantly refutes a charge made by the
pagan historian Zosimus that this tax was devised by Constantine,[3]
but he does not tell us whether Anastasius emulated Philip by
suppressing the profession upon whose gains it was levied.

---

[1] Transl. from Clyde Pharr, op. cit., p. 232.
[2] *Hist. Eccl.* iii. 39.   [3] Ibid., iii. 40–41.

Probably the emperor contented himself with renouncing the revenue derived from such a disreputable source, while ignoring the abuse itself which had proved so lucrative to the treasury.

Although positive proof is lacking, there is doubtless some truth in the common assertion[1] that the interpretative extensions of the Julian law and the legislation of the Theodosian Code relative to homosexual practices were never rigidly enforced. Certainly Justinian seems to have felt that new and stringent measures were necessary, for he published two *novellæ* denouncing unnatural lusts in stern and pious language, and threatening obdurate sodomists with the fullest rigours of the law. These edicts have particular interest, not only in themselves, but because the juristic fame of their promulgator has invested them with a special authority, with the result that they have exerted a strong influence upon the formation of mediæval and modern opinion, and have tended to standardize punishments of extreme severity.

The first of these *novellæ*, against homosexual acts and blasphemy, was issued in 538, and the following portions are relevant to our study:

NOV. 77: '. . . since certain men, seized by diabolical incitement, practise among themselves the most disgraceful lusts, and act contrary to nature: we enjoin them to take to heart the fear of God and the judgement to come, and to abstain from suchlike diabolical and unlawful lusts, so that they may not be visited by the just wrath of God on account of these impious acts, with the result that cities perish with all their inhabitants. For we are taught by the Holy Scriptures that because of like impious conduct cities have indeed perished, together with the men in them. §1 . . .[2] . . . For because of such crimes[3] there are famines, earthquakes, and pestilences; wherefore we admonish men to abstain from the aforesaid unlawful acts, that they may not lose their souls. But if, after this our admonition,

---

[1] See, e.g., Ellis, op. cit., ii, p. 346; J. A. Symonds, op. cit., p. 8.

[2] There follows a section condemning various blasphemies—swearing "by God's hairs", or "by God's head", and the like.

[3] It is not clear whether this refers only to the blasphemies, or to homosexual practices as well.

any are found persisting in such offences, first, they render themselves unworthy of the mercy of God, and then they are subjected to
the punishment enjoined by the law. § 2. For we order the most
illustrious prefect of the Capital to arrest those who persist in the
aforesaid[1] lawless and impious acts after they have been warned by us,
and to inflict on them the extreme punishments, so that the city and
the state may not come to harm by reason of such wicked deeds. And
if, after this our warning, any be found who have concealed their
crime, they shall likewise be condemned by the Lord God. And if the
most illustrious prefect find any who have committed any such
offence, and shall omit to punish them according to our laws, first, he
will be liable to the judgement of God, and he will also incur our
indignation.'

Six years later this was followed by the second edict, dated 15th
March 544, and directed solely against homosexual practices:

NOV. 141: 'Preamble: Though we stand always in need of the
kindness and goodness of God, yet is this specially the case at this
time, when in various ways we have provoked him to anger on
account of the multitude of our sins. And although he has warned us,
and has shown us clearly what we deserve because of our offences,
yet he has acted mercifully towards us and, awaiting our penitence,
has reserved his wrath for other times—for he has "no pleasure in
the death of the wicked; but that the wicked turn from his way and
live". Wherefore it is not right that we should all despise God's
abundant goodness, forbearance, and longsuffering kindness and,
hardening our hearts and turning away from penitence, should heap
upon ourselves wrath in the day of wrath. Rather, we ought to
abstain from all base concerns and acts—and especially does this
apply to such as have gone to decay through that abominable and
impious conduct deservedly hated by God. We speak of the defilement of males (*de stupro masculorum*) which some men sacrilegiously
and impiously dare to attempt, perpetrating vile acts with other men.
  § I. For, instructed by the Holy Scriptures, we know that God
brought a just judgement upon those who lived in Sodom, on
account of this very madness of intercourse, so that to this very day
that land burns with inextinguishable fire. By this God teaches us, in

---

[1] This almost certainly refers to both unnatural lusts and blasphemies.

order that by means of legislation we may avert such an untoward fate. Again, we know what the blessed Apostle says about such things, and what laws[1] our state enacts. Wherefore it behoves all who desire to fear God to abstain from conduct so base and criminal that we do not find it committed even by brute beasts. Let those who have not taken part in such doings continue to refrain in the future. But as for those who have been consumed by this kind of disease, let them not only cease to sin in the future, but let them also duly do penance, and fall down before God and renounce their plague [in confession] to the blessed Patriarch; let them understand the reason for this charge and, as it is written, bring forth the fruits of repentance. So may God the merciful, in the abundance of his pity, deem us worthy of his blessing, that we may all give thanks to him for the salvation of the penitents, whom we have now bidden [to submit themselves] in order that the magistrates too may follow up our action, [thus] reconciling to themselves God who is justly angry with us. And we also, wisely and prudently having in reverence the sacred season, entreat God the merciful that those who have been contaminated by the filth of this impious conduct may strive for penitence, that we may not have to prosecute this crime on another occasion. Next, we proclaim to all who are conscious that they have committed any such sin, that unless they desist and, renouncing it [in confession] before the blessed Patriarch, take care for their salvation, placating God during the holy season for such impious acts, they will bring upon themselves severer penalties, even though on other counts they are held guilty of no fault. For there will be no relaxation of enquiry and correction so far as this matter is concerned, nor will they be dealt with carelessly who do not submit themselves during the time of the holy season, or who persist in such impious conduct, lest if we are negligent we arouse God's anger against us. If, with eyes as it were blinded, we overlook such impious and forbidden conduct, we may provoke the good God to anger and bring ruin upon all—a fate which would be but deserved.'

These edicts are distinguished from previous enactments by a sententious and hortatory tone characteristic of their author, and

---

[1] That is, presumably, the *Lex Julia* as extended by the interpretations of the jurists, *Cod. Theodos.* IX. vii. 3 and 6, and *Nov.* 77.

they present several new and interesting features. But in one respect they possess no novelty; contrary to the common opinion, they state no new penalties and create no new crimes, but simply direct the enforcement of the existing laws against homosexual practices. *Novella* 77 does no more than enjoin the guilty to abandon their unnatural lusts, warning them that if they fail to heed the imperial admonition they will be arrested and the prescribed punishments will be inflicted. *Novella* 141, issued during Lent, appropriately demands not only renunciation of homosexual practices, but also repentance and confession. But those who do not amend their ways are again threatened with the rigours of the law, and it appears as if some investigation was being conducted by the authorities—possibly into the prostitution of the *exsoleti* which was undoubtedly flourishing some thirty years before, and against which both *novellæ* may have been specially directed.

The chief motive behind the laws of 538 and 544 is plainly stated. Homosexual acts endanger the state, for they are liable (as the Scriptures testify) to provoke the vengeance of God in the form of earthquake, famine, and pestilence; therefore it is the duty of the legislator to protect the community by statutes heavily penalizing such impious conduct. Yet sodomists are not condemned out of hand, for the Christian emperor exhorts them to penitence and reformation; only if they reject the way of repentance and the grace of forgiveness does it appear that the laws are to be invoked against them. This concern that sinners shall turn again and seek salvation, particularly during the holy season of Lent, is something which the critics of the "fanatical" and "bigoted" Justinian pass over in silence; yet it argues a commendable reluctance to enforce the civil law, with its extreme penalties, so long as the offender does not spurn the discipline of the Church by means of which he may be brought to amendment of life.

In these two *novellæ* we see clearly the influence of the homosexual interpretation of the Sodom story, threatening with dire calamities all those who practise unnatural lusts. But it is improbable that this legislation was motivated merely by vague fears that another such act of divine retribution might occur. During the previous reign the year 525 had been marked by terrible earthquakes and floods which devastated the cities of Edessa, Anazarba, and Pompeiopolis in the East, and Corinth and Dyrrachium in Europe; while at the same time Antioch was destroyed by fire and inundation. It may well have been the recollection of this disastrous time which made Justinian apprehensive lest such catastrophes might be a warning of the judgement impending over his capital because of its vices.

This perhaps explains the reason for the issue of the edict of 538. For that of 544 a cause can be assigned with much greater certainty. In the previous year a great plague had swept through Constantinople, and it was doubtless with this in mind that Justinian took occasion during the following Lent to summon to repentance those in particular whose practices might (according to current belief) provoke other and possibly more dreadful consequences. It was only natural, considering the opinion of the time, that any serious epidemic should be regarded as a warning of the fate of Sodom no less than earthquake and flood; every such disaster was liable to be interpreted as a divine visitation for sin, of which the overthrow of the cities of the Plain stood as the classic example. Hence the almost inevitable assumption that homosexual practices were the cause (mainly or exclusively) of God's wrath: hence, too, the emperor's call to repentance, for what the law punished as a crime the Scriptures denounced as sin—yet the Lord had declared by Ezekiel the prophet: 'As I live ... I have no pleasure in the death of the wicked, but that the wicked turn from his way and live'.[1] These words form, as it were, the theme of Justinian's edict; only if the sinners persist in their iniquity will it be necessary to invoke the statutes which exist to restrain the evil-doer, and so to avert from the state by legal compulsion a destruction like that of Sodom and Gomorrah.

One further point calls for comment. It has been assumed by

---

[1] Ez. xxxiii. 11, quoted in *Nov.* 141.

some that Justinian intended to discriminate between habitual and occasional homosexual practice, and to punish only the former.[1] It is by no means clear on what this opinion is based, but it is perhaps attributable to the apparent distinction in *novella* 141 between 'those who have been consumed (*contabuerunt*) by this kind of disease', and 'all who are conscious that they have committed any such sin'. It is very doubtful, however, whether these phrases (or indeed any others in either *novella*) actually imply any such discrimination. Certainly no variation in penalty is indicated, but all alike are enjoined to do penance, and are reminded of the laws which the state has enacted. It is difficult to see why there should be any such discrimination, since it would hardly appear to serve any useful purpose. It is most unlikely that Justinian would have adopted so clumsy and vague a method of separating *exsoleti* from other offenders; and we cannot suppose (as perhaps the proponents of this view intended to suggest) that there was in the emperor's mind any distinction so anachronistic as that which might be drawn today between the homosexual acts of the genuine invert and those, say, of a heterosexual pervert engaging in prostitution.

We have no reliable contemporary evidence of the extent to which Justinian's legislation succeeded in enforcing the law against homosexual practices. Gibbon hints at perversions of justice in which 'pæderasty became the crime of those to whom no crime could be imputed',[2] insinuating that the laws punishing sodomy were often invoked for political reasons; but of this there is no proof, and Gibbon offers none. He himself only quotes one instance of the application of the statutes—that of the chastisement and disgrace of two bishops, Isaiah of Rhodes and Alexander of Diospolis, who, *resecta siquidem virile caule, per urbem ignominiose traducti sunt;*[3] but this happened, according to Theophanes, in 521—prior both to the reign of Justinian and to the issue of

---

[1] Cf. Ellis, op. cit., ii, p. 347, n. 2.

[2] E. Gibbon, *The History of the Decline and Fall of the Roman Empire* (ed. J. B. Bury, London, 1898, 7 vols.), iv, p. 506.

[3] Theophanes, *Chronographia,* A.C. 521 (Migne, *Patr. Græc.,* cviii, col. 407).

novellæ 77 and 141. Castration, followed by public exhibition of the offender, was certainly one of the penalties inflicted for sodomy, so Procopius tells us;[1] and he also refers to 'a certain intolerable punishment',[2] which may be that described by Gibbon—'the insertion of sharp reeds into the pores and tubes of most exquisite sensibility'.[3] It seems probable that such barbarous punishments were inflicted in commutation of the death penalty, but there is no evidence to show that they were applied with any frequency, or in other than special cases; in fact, the imperial edicts against homosexual practices appear to have been no less obscure in their operation than the earlier *Lex Scantinia*.

So much, then, for the "veritable crusade" against homosexual practices attributed by Westermarck to the Christian emperors. On investigation, we find that it amounts simply to the issue of four edicts in two hundred years—the last being mainly a call to repentance. None of these enactments, so far as the evidence goes, seems to have been implemented by any vigorous or sustained campaign to suppress sodomy or to exterminate the pæderast; if such a "crusade" had been undertaken, we may suppose that it would have been mentioned in the records of the time, or at least would not have escaped the attention of annalists and gossip writers. That no such campaign was instituted does not, of course, argue any negligence or want of moral zeal on the part of Valentinian and his colleagues and of Justinian,[4] in their efforts to extirpate what they sincerely believed to be a social danger no less than a grievous sin. But the picture, conjured up by certain writers, of panic-stricken imperial religious fanatics obsessed with fear of the consequences of sodomy and committed by their Faith to an implacable persecution of the "love" which the Greeks had esteemed, is a mischievous travesty of the facts. On the contrary, the edicts of the emperors (with the possible exception of the curious statute issued by Constantius and Constans in

---

[1] *Anecd.* xi. 36.   [2] Ibid., xvi. 20.
[3] Op. cit., iv, p. 505.
[4] Disregarding the ambiguous edict put forth by Constantius and Constans, which there may have been no intention to implement.

342) were the acts of responsible legislators and, like the interpretative extensions of the *Lex Julia de adulteriis* framed by the great
jurists, were directed against abuses which are incontestably
injurious to the well-being of society.

Of these abuses, the two chief were the corruption of boys and
the practice of male homosexual prostitution. Tradition had
always connected the earliest law against unnatural crime, the
Lex Scantinia, with a notorious case involving the young
M. Claudius Marcellus; and the decisions of Papinian and Paulus
that *stuprum* included offences against boys, and was a capital
crime when committed with a *puer prætextatus,* were aimed at the
protection of minors. The emperor Philip suppressed the *exsoleti,*
Marcianus held that the loan of premises for the purpose of committing *stuprum cum masculo* was a criminal offence, and both
edicts in the Theodosian Code (whatever else their purpose)
render homosexual prostitution illegal and punishable.

Justinian, who is often castigated as the chief and most
fanatical of the Christian emperors who penalized homosexual
practices, is in fact notable as the only one who showed himself
concerned as much for the repentance and reformation of
offenders as for their punishment. In both his *novellæ* he first
called upon sodomists to desist from their impious practices, that
they might not lose their souls, and made it clear that the sentence
of the law was reserved only for the obdurate who spurned God's
merciful offer of forgiveness extended to all who are truly penitent and desire to amend their lives. Moreover he did not, as it has
been alleged, revive 'the laws of primitive morality that had
first been drawn up for the exclusive use of the Children of
Israel'[1]—that is to say, the enactments against homosexual
practices in the Holiness Code of Leviticus. He simply attempted
to enforce the legislation of his predecessors, endorsing in the
process the opinions of the pagan jurisconsults, and his sole innova-
tion (apart from urging offenders to repent) was to emphasize his

---

[1] D. Stanley-Jones, op. cit., p. 18; cf. p. 20: 'The edict of Justinian . . . holds a
key position as the link between the Mosaic Code and the present law . . .'

appeals and warnings by a reminder of the fate of Sodom—thus for the first time introducing the reinterpreted Sodom story as a justification for legal measures against those who indulged in homosexual acts. Finally, while it may truly be said that Justinian, through his *novellæ* and his codification of the law, played a considerable part in determining the Western Christian attitude towards homosexual practices, it is often forgotten that no less important an influence was exerted by the edict of Valentinian, Theodosius, and Arcadius, which was incorporated into both the *Codex Theodosianus* and the *Codex Justinianus*.

IV

LEGISLATION, TEACHING, AND OPINION IN THE CHURCH

1. Patristic Thought

UNDERLYING the attitude of the early Church to homosexual practices there was, of course, the belief (now firmly established) that they had been specially condemned by God in the overthrow of Sodom and Gomorrah. Nevertheless, such practices were generally denounced mainly on the ground that they are in themselves unnatural. Thus Tertullian clearly has such vices as pæderasty in mind when he writes: '... all other frenzies of the lusts which exceed the laws of nature and are impious towards both [human] bodies and the sexes we banish, not only from the threshold but also from all shelter of the Church, for they are not sins so much as monstrosities';[1] and in these words, though they belong to his Montanist period, he speaks for catholics no less than for those of his own sect. Likewise the *Apostolical Constitutions* declare that Christians 'abhor all unlawful mixtures, and that which is practised by some contrary to nature, as wicked and impious'[2]

John Chrysostom is particularly emphatic in denouncing homosexual practices as unnatural. Commenting upon Rom. i. 26–27,[3] he observes that all genuine pleasure is according to

---

[1] *De pudic.* iv.

[2] *Const. Apost.* vi. 11; cf. vi. 28.

[3] *In epist. ad Rom.* iv, where homosexual practices are dealt with at length (cf. also *in epist. ad Tit.* v. 4); here I have only noted some of the points bearing directly upon the matter under discussion.

nature;[1] the delights of sodomy, on the other hand, are an unpardonable insult to nature, while tribadism is even more disgraceful, for women ought to have more shame than men. Such immoralities are doubly destructive; they jeopardize the race by deflecting the sexual organs from their primary procreative purpose, and they sow disharmony and strife between man and woman, who are no longer impelled by their physical desires to live peaceably together. Fornication, though certainly lawless, is at least natural, but sodomy and lesbianism are in every respect inordinate.[2]

In exposing the vices of paganism Christian moralists do not fail to point out that when homosexual acts are attributed to gods and heroes,[3] it is hardly surprising that men should imitate the example of Zeus and Ganymede.[4] At a very early date the *Didache* and the *Epistle of Barnabas* contain the injunction: 'Thou shalt not corrupt boys (*ou paidophthorēseis*)',[5] which appears later in the three versions of the *Sahidic Heptateuch*,[6] while John Chrysostom, in one of his sermons, inveighs against the pæderasts who come to church to look with lustful curiosity upon handsome youths.[7] Augustine contends that homosexual practices are transgressions of the command to love God and one's neighbour, and declares that '. . . those shameful acts against nature, such as were committed in Sodom, ought everywhere and always to be detested and punished. If all nations were to do such things, they would [equally] be held guilty of the same crime by the law of God, which has not so made men that they should use one another in this way'.[8] Indeed, sodomy is to him a bodily defilement, and

---

[1] Cf. *in epist. ad Rom.* ix—natural pleasure is always greater than pleasure sought unnaturally.

[2] For other condemnations of homosexual practices, see Justin, *I Apol.* xxvii; Eusebius, *Theoph.* ii. 81 and *Demonstr. evang.* iv. 10; Lactantius, *Instit.* v. 9; and Salvian, *De gubernat. Dei,* vii. 7.

[3] Cf. Arnobius, *Adv. gent.* v. 6–7; Clem. Alex., *Cohort. ad gent.* ii; Cyprian, *Epist.* i (*ad Don.*).

[4] Cf. Eusebius, *Theoph.* ii. 15.   [5] *Didache,* ii. 2; *Epist. Barn.* xix. 4.

[6] *Eth.* 4, *Arab.* 4, *Sahid.* 6; cf. *Didascalia Apost.* 1.

[7] *In Matt. hom.* lxxiii. 3.   [8] *Conf.* III. viii [15].

to avoid being compelled to submit to it, a lie is permissible,[1] provided it does not violate 'the doctrine of piety, nor piety itself, nor innocence, nor benevolence'.[2]

Certain writers actually discover in the natural history of their time an argument against homosexual practices. There was among the ancients a curious belief that every year the hare acquires an additional anus, and that the resultant superabundance of bodily orifices accounts for the supposedly lustful propensities of this prolific animal. This, says Clement of Alexandria, explains why Moses prohibited the use of the hare as food;[3] by declaring it unclean, he implicitly condemned all unnatural modes of coitus, and especially *paiderastia*.[4] Novatian likewise states that the hare 'rebukes men *deformatos in feminam*',[5] while the author of the *Epistle of Barnabas* bases his injunction: 'Thou shalt not be found a corrupter of boys (*paidophthoros*)',[6] upon the prohibition in the Law against eating the flesh of this creature.

It is evident that the practices chiefly denounced in these and other passages are simply active and passive sodomy, particularly in the form of *paidophthoria*. In the *Epistle of Barnabas*, however, *fellatio* is also condemned[7]—again, as a result of an interpretation of the Jewish Law in terms of the natural history of antiquity; according to the author, the weasel is pronounced unclean in Leviticus because it is reputed to conceive through its mouth.[8] In the *Octavius*, Minucius Felix also mentions *fellatio*, and perhaps also homosexual *cunnilingus* (that is, as practised by one woman with another)[9]—though in the case of the latter, the passage may refer to heterosexual rather than to homosexual acts.

Even the monastic life was apparently not without its temptations to indulge in homosexual practices, and a passage in Basil's treatise, *De renuntiatione sæculi* is of special interest. No doubt his warnings were not unnecessary in the case of recent converts,

---

[1] *De mend.* ix [15].   [2] Ibid., xx [41].
[3] Deut. xiv. 7.   [4] *Pæd.* ii. 10.
[5] *De cib. Jud. epist.* 3.   [6] *Epist. Barn.* x. 6.
[7] *Epist. Barn.* x. 8; heterosexual *fellatio* is also condemned in the same place.
[8] Lev. xi. 29.   [9] *Oct.* 28.

and they bring vividly before us a feature of contemporary social life which may seem strange, if not fantastic, to the modern reader:

'If thou art young in either body or mind, shun the companionship of other young men and avoid them as thou wouldest a flame. For through them the enemy has kindled the desires of many and then handed them over to eternal fire, hurling them into the vile pit of the five cities under the pretence of spiritual love. . . . At meals take a seat far from other young men. In lying down to sleep let not their clothes be near thine, but rather have an old man between you. When a young man converses with thee, or sings psalms facing thee, answer him with eyes cast down, lest perhaps by gazing at his face thou receive a seed of desire sown by the enemy and reap sheaves of corruption and ruin. Whether in the house or in a place where there is no one to see your actions, be not found in his company under the pretence either of studying the divine oracles or of any other business whatever, however necessary.'[1]

From a letter written in 423 by Augustine to some nuns over whom his sister had been Superior we would infer that similar dangers attended the life of a woman in monastic communities:

EPIST. ccxi. 14: 'The love which you bear to one another ought not to be carnal, but spiritual: for those things which are practised by immodest women, even with other females, in shameful jesting and playing, ought not to be done even by married women or by girls who are about to marry, much less by the widows or chaste virgins dedicated by a holy vow to be the handmaids of Christ.'

Although the matter is never discussed extensively, nor in general otherwise than incidentally, there can be no doubt that the early Church regarded homosexual practices with unqualified disapproval, particularly when committed by men with boys, or with one another. The ecclesiastical legislation which we must now review reflects this attitude, and shows what steps were taken to penalize offenders by imposing spiritual punishments.

---

[1] Transl., W. K. L. Clarke, *The Ascetic Works of Saint Basil* (London, 1925), p. 66.

2. ENACTMENTS OF COUNCILS AND SYNODS, CANON LAW, AND ECCLESIASTICAL REGULATIONS

Some of the earliest references to homosexual practices occur in the Church Orders, which include sodomists among the persons who are to be debarred, not only from baptism but even from admission to the catechumenate and to instruction in the faith, until they have renounced their evil ways.[1] At the beginning of the fourth century the Council of Elvira (305–306), in southern Spain, included among its voluminous enactments a canon which forbade the admission of *stupratores puerorum* to the Communion, even when at death's door.[2] It is most unlikely, however, that the censure of the Church was reserved solely for those who, after baptism, continued unrepentantly their addiction to the "love of boys"; no doubt the canon in question was framed with a particular situation in view, but subsequent legislation and Church opinion suggests that at this time no distinction was made between different kinds of homosexual offenders.

A few years later, at the Council of Ancyra in Asia Minor (314), two canons were passed which require examination in some detail. Both these canons[3] penalize certain persons termed *alogeusamenoi*, that is, those who are guilty of shamelessly offensive conduct; but the precise significance of this word is not immediately apparent from the text of the rules themselves, and the first hints as to their connotation are found in certain ancient Latin interpretations. The first, *Interpretatio "Prisca"*, entitles the canons thus:[4]

> CAN. 16:[5] 'Concerning those who have committed fornication with animals.'

---

[1] See the *Apostolical Tradition* of Hippolytus, II. xvi. 20; the *Canons of Hippolytus*, 76; the *Sahidic Heptateuch—Eth.* 29 (? and 63), *Arab.* 28 (? and 62), *Sahid.* 75 (and 41?); the *Testament of the Lord*, ii. 2.

[2] *Conc. Illib.* 71.

[3] *Conc. Ancyr.* 16 and 17.

[4] For the Latin text, see C. H. Turner, *Ecclesiæ Occidentalis Monumenta Juris Antiquissima* (Oxford, 1909 f.), ii. p. 19.

[5] Numbered 15 in the *Interpretationes*.

CAN. 17:[1] 'Concerning those who either have been defiled or commit defilement (*aut corrupti sunt aut corrumpunt*) with animals or with males (*in masculis*).'

In the text itself of canon 17 the word *alogeusamenoi* is rendered by the phrase, 'those who become corrupt(*fraciscunt*)[2] [by acting] as animals with animals, or [by defiling themselves] with males (*in masculis*)' [3]—that is to say, both the headings provided by the Interpreter, and the Latin versions of the text, suggest that canon 16 is directed against bestiality, and canon 17 against both bestiality and sodomy.

A second exposition, the Isidorian (which exists in two forms), reverses the interpretations of the "*Prisca*". Both the *Interpretatio Isidori antiqua* and the *Interpretatio Isidori vulgata* treat canon 17 as a law against bestiality only,[4] and regard canon 16 as having the wider reference. But in their interpretation of the latter, the *antiqua* and the *vulgata* differ. The *antiqua* extends still further the significance of *alogeusamenoi* by assigning to it a triple meaning; it denotes 'those who have been joined in coitus with beasts, or after the manner of beasts have committed incest with their near kindred, or have lain with males'. The *vulgata*, however, omits the last clause (relating to sodomy), thus restricting the application of the canon to bestiality and incest (or, perhaps, unions within the prohibited degrees of relationship).[5]

Yet a third interpretation, that of Dionysius Exiguus, exhibits certain variations from those already considered. Like the Isidorian, it is found in two versions. Both agree with the "*Prisca*" (as against the *antiqua* and the *vulgata* of Isidore) in regarding canon 17 as directed against bestiality and sodomy, though in their wording they differ slightly but unimportantly.[6] On the other hand, while the Dionysian *Interpretatio I* accords with the

---

[1] Numbered 16 in the *Interpretationes*.
[2] Probably an attempt to render what the Interpreter took to be the sense of *leprōsantas* in the original.
[3] See C. H. Turner, op. cit., ii, p. 25 for the Latin text.
[4] Ibid., ii, p. 100.
[5] Ibid., ii, pp. 92–94.   [6] Ibid., ii, p. 101.

Isidorian *antiqua* in attaching to *alogeusamenoi* in canon 16 a three-fold significance ('those who have had sexual intercourse with beasts, or have committed incest with blood relations, or have been contaminated with males'), the *Interpretatio II* disagrees with both the *"Prisca"* and the two Isidorian interpretations in treating this canon as directed against bestiality and sodomy.[1]

In spite of these various inconsistencies, the effect of the Latin interpretations of canons 16 and 17 of the Council of Ancyra was to establish the view that either one or both these enactments applied to those who had been guilty of homosexual practices. To such persons, therefore, the stated penalties appertained. Under canon 16 penances of varying duration and severity were imposed, according to whether the offender was under or over twenty years of age, whether his indulgence was habitual or not, and whether he was single or married; if he was married, and over fifty years old, he might only be admitted to the Communion when at the point of death. Under canon 17, the sinner was excluded from the church and was compelled to remain outside with penitents of the lowest class.

The influence of these interpretations upon the Church in the West is to be seen in the fact that canons 16 and 17 of the Council of Ancyra (and especially the former) are cited as authoritative in subsequent enactments against homosexual practices.[2] Moreover, the provisions of canon 16 may well have inspired or affected to some extent the later attempts, in the Penitentials and elsewhere, to discriminate between different homosexual offences and offenders. Nevertheless, there is no doubt that the original legislation itself bears no reference whatever to homosexual practices—nor, indeed, to incest. It is now generally accepted that the term *alogeusamenoi* denotes those men who have committed

---

[1] See C. H. Turner, op. cit., ii, pp. 93–95.

[2] Cf. *Capit. Aquisgran.* (789), 48 (see J. Mansi, *Sacr. Concil. . . . Collectio,* Venice, 1759 ff.; facsimile reproduction, Paris and Leipzig, 1901 ff., xvii b, col. 230, for text); *Capit. Carol. mag.* 48 (Mansi, op. cit., xvii b, col. 710); *Capit. Carol. mag. et Ludovic. pii,* v. 82 (Mansi, op. cit., xvii b, col. 839); vii. 351 (Mansi, op. cit., xvii b, col. 1101); *Canones Isaac episc. Lingonen.* iv. 11 (Mansi, op. cit., xvii b, col. 1259); *Conc. Paris.* (829), i. 34 (Mansi, op. cit., xiv, col. 560).

immoral sexual acts with animals;[1] consequently, while due allowance must be made for the part played by the Latin *Interpretationes* in forming the Church's attitude to homosexual acts, the Greek canons in question must be regarded as irrelevant to our study, and inadmissible as evidence of the view of the Church in the fourth century.

Some indication of opinion in the East towards the close of this century, however, is given by the disciplinary regulations of Basil and Gregory of Nyssa. In his third canonical letter to Amphilochius, bishop of Iconium, written in 375, Basil lays down the following rule:

> EPIST. ccxvii, can. 62: 'He who is guilty of unseemliness with males (*tēn aschēmosunēn en tois arrhesin*) will be under discipline for the same time as adulterers.'

Gregory, in his canonical letter to Letoius, bishop of Melitene, probably composed about the year 390, explains the reason for treating sodomists in the same way as adulterers. The more subtle thinkers, he says, are inclined to regard adultery as equivalent to fornication, since in both cases use is made of what is not one's own—and certainly the two sins are not markedly different in character. But a simpler distinction is possible: while fornication is the indulgence of sexual lust without doing injury to another, adultery always involves treachery and wrong against someone else. In the latter category bestiality and *paiderastia* must also be placed, for neither union with an alien kind nor homosexual coitus can occur without the commission of injustice. Being, therefore, of a like nature to adultery, both copulation with beasts and raging desire for males (*hē kata tous arrhenas lussa*) merit a double penalty, as compared with fornication, for each is doubly sinful in that it combines an unlawful pleasure with the infliction of injury upon another.[2]

According to Basil, the penance for adulterers (and therefore for sodomists, as for those guilty of bestiality) was exclusion from

---

[1] See C. J. Hefele, transl. and ed. H. Leclercq, etc., *Histoire des Conciles* (Paris 1907 ff.), I, i, p. 318.

[2] *Epist. canonica,* 4.

the Sacrament for fifteen years, that allotted to fornicators being only seven years.[1] During the first four years the penitent took his place with the *prosklaiontes* or "mourners", who stood in the open area outside the church door, cut off from all participation in the sacred rites, clad in a garb appropriate to their condition, and making frequent and public confession of their sin. This initial stage accomplished, he joined the *akroōmenoi* or "hearers", who were allowed to come within the porch of the church (or into the narthex), and were able to hear the Scriptures and the sermon, but did not receive any imposition of hands or share in the intercessions. After five years spent thus, he passed another four among the *hupopiptontes* or "kneelers", now recognized again as a member of the Christian community, but distinguished by a special dress and required to undergo certain acts of self-mortification. Finally, the long period of discipline was completed by two years with the *sunistamenoi* or "bystanders", who worshipped in church with the faithful, but probably sat in a place apart from the rest of the congregation.[2]

Gregory's penitential system was less rigorous than Basil's; the delinquent was required to pass three years in each of the first three stages, but no mention is made of his being a "bystander". It is doubtful whether the full period of fifteen or nine years was always (or ever) imposed upon sodomists. It seems that offenders might often begin their penance as "hearers"—total exclusion from church being a penalty generally held in reserve—and the strictness of the discipline as a whole was probably relaxed in many cases; indeed, Gregory concludes his injunctions regarding adultery, fornication, bestiality, and *paiderastia* by stating expressly that discretion is to be used in imposing penances, while Basil says that the bishop may exercise his power of binding and loosing in favour of an earnest penitent.[3]

---

[1] *Epist.* ccxvii (*ad Amphiloch.*), 58, 59, 63.

[2] For details of the penitential system in the ancient Church, see G. Mead, art. "Penitence", in W. Smith and S. Cheetham, *A Dictionary of Christian Antiquities* (London, 1876–1880), ii, pp. 1591–1596.

[3] *Epist.* ccxvii. 74.

It can hardly be said that the spiritual penalties imposed by these Eastern canons upon men guilty of homosexual practices are marked by an excessive harshness; in fact, they compare favourably in this respect with the discipline required in the extreme West by the Council of Elvira.[1] Basil certainly regards sodomy as a grave sin, and treats it with the same severity as adultery, bestiality, fornication by a monk or a nun, and incest with any woman other than a sister; yet he deals with it more leniently than with murder, divination and conjuration, incest with a sister (all incurring a penance of twenty years), and apostasy (which was punished by exclusion from Communion until the hour of death). According to Gregory's code the impositions are generally lighter, but the sodomist is again requited less heavily than the murderer (who is to do penance for periods ranging from fifteen to twenty-seven years, according to circumstances) and the apostate (who receives the same punishment as in Basil's code).

During the following centuries legislation against homosexual practices is not abundant, and much of what exists is repetitive and wanting in special interest. Select examples will, therefore, suffice to indicate the general attitude of the Church and of the Christian prince.

A canon of the second Council of Tours (567) enforces the regulation in the Rule of St Benedict[2] that monks must not sleep two in a bed, and extends it to priests also, in order that no evil suspicions may arise[3]—but there is nothing to indicate that this canon was rendered necessary by any outbreak of homosexual practices as a result of such sleeping arrangements. Similar enactments are found later,[4] including one by a council held at Paris in 1212 which forbids nuns as well as monks to sleep together, and applies to nunnery dormitories the provision of the Benedictine Rule[5] which orders lamps to be burning throughout the night.[6]

---

[1] See above, p. 86. [2] Cf. ch. 22. [3] *Conc. II Turon.* 14.
[4] Cf. *Conc. I Aquisgran.* (816), and the *Regula Canonicorum* of Chrodogang, bishop of Metz.
[5] Cf. again ch. 22.
[6] *Conc. Paris.* (1212), ii. 21; iii. 2 (see Mansi, op. cit., xxii, coll. 831, 834).

The same prohibitions, obviously copied from the canons of this council, occur among the regulations of a council held in 1214 at Rheims;[1] both these assemblies will require further consideration later.[2]

The kings and Church councils of Gothic Spain addressed themselves with energy to the suppression of homosexual practices. Kindasvinth, who reigned from 642 to 653 and introduced many reforms and a much-needed uniformity into the Gothic law, issued an edict about the year 650 which ran as follows:

LEX VISIGOTH. III. v. 4: 'That crime which ought always to be detested, and is regarded as an execrable moral depravity, ought not to be left unavenged. Therefore those who lie with males, or who consent to participate passively in such acts, ought to be smitten by the sentence of this law—namely, that as soon as an offence has been admitted and the judge has publicly investigated it, he should forthwith take steps to have offenders of both kinds castrated. Then he should hand them over to the bishop of the district where the offence happens to have been committed, so that by his authority those who are known to have perpetrated such unlawful acts voluntarily may be subjected to forcible expulsion[3] if they show themselves reluctant to undergo punishment[4] for what they have done. Meanwhile, if anyone is known to have performed this horrible and disgraceful act unwillingly and not voluntarily, whether he was active (*inferens*) or passive (*patiens*), then he can be held free of guilt if he comes forward himself to reveal the base crime. But the man who is well known to have sunk to this madness of his own free will is undoubtedly liable to punishment. And if those who have consented to do such acts have wives, their sons or legitimate heirs can obtain possession of their property; while as for the wife, when she has received for her own portion sufficient for a dowry, and has retained her own belongings intact, she shall remain unquestionably and absolutely free to marry whom she wills.'[5]

---

[1] *Conc. Rotomag.* (1214), ii. 23, 32 (see Mansi, op. cit., xxii, coll. 910, 912).

[2] See pp. 127–135.

[3] Either excommunication or banishment is probably meant.

[4] I.e., penance—the legal penalty of castration having already been inflicted.

[5] Text in *Monumenta Germaniæ Historica: Legum sectio I, Leg. nat. Germ.*, I (Hanover and Leipzig, 1902), p. 163.

Perhaps this law was insufficiently enforced or otherwise ineffective, for some forty years later Egica, one of Kindasvinth's successors, in his opening speech to the sixteenth council of Toledo (693), urged the assembled clergy and *viri illustres* to address themselves to the curbing of homosexual practices: 'Among other matters, see that you determine to extirpate that obscene crime committed by those who lie with males, whose fearful conduct defiles the charm of honest living and provokes from heaven the wrath of the supreme Judge'.[1] Obedient to the royal behest, the council enacted that in view of the prevalence of sodomy,

CONC. XVI TOLETAN. 3: '. . . if any one of those males who commit this vile practice against nature with other males is a bishop, a priest, or a deacon, he shall be degraded from the dignity of his order, and shall remain in perpetual exile, struck down by damnation. Moreover, if any have been implicated in the evils of another's filthy doings, let them be punished none the less, without respect of order, rank, or person, by the sentence of that law[2] which was enacted concerning such offences, and let them be excluded from all communion with Christians, and furthermore let them be punished with one hundred stripes of the lash, shorn of their hair as a mark of disgrace, and banished in perpetual exile . . .'[3]

This canon Egica himself supplemented with the following edict:

LEX VISIGOTH. III. v. 7: 'We are compelled by the teaching of the orthodox faith to impose the censure of the law upon indecent practices, and to restrain with the bridle of continence those who have been involved in lapses of the flesh. For we best serve the interests of our people and country with clemency and piety when we take care both to root out completely crimes of depravity, and to bring to an end evil acts of vice. Certainly we strive to abolish the detestable outrage of that lust by the filthy uncleanness of which men do not fear to defile other men in the unlawful act of sodomy (*stuprum*); as often, therefore, as they pollute themselves by the

---

[1] Text in *Mon. Germ. Hist.,* op. cit., p. 483—*Tomus Egicani Regis concilio* [*Toletan.*] *oblatus,* which is, without doubt, the *tomus* delivered to the sixteenth council of Toledo.

[2] *Lex Visigoth.* III. v. 4.

[3] For the text, see Mansi, op cit., xii, col. 71.

mutual defilement of this crime, we regard their conduct as an offence against both divine religion and chastity. Athough indeed both the authority of Holy Scripture and the decree of the secular law prohibit absolutely this kind of delinquency, nevertheless it is necessary to repeal that statute[1] by a new enactment lest, while the time for amendment is deferred, worse vices are seen to spring up. Therefore by this edict and law we decree that from this time forward and hereafter if any man, be he cleric or layman, whatever his state or birth, is clearly detected (by whatever evidence) in the crime aforesaid, let him thereupon not only endure castration by command of the prince or the direction of the person judging the case, but let him also undergo the extreme penalty for these offences which the canon passed lately (that is to say, in the third year of our reign[2]) by ecclesiastical decree plainly lays down.'[3]

There seems to be no obvious explanation for this vigorous severity on the part of the kings of Gothic Spain towards those who were guilty of indulgence in homosexual acts. When we take into account the circumstances of the time, however, it becomes by no means improbable that Kindasvinth and Egica promulgated their edicts for political as well as moral reasons. For the removal of an inconvenient opponent few charges might be so plausible and effective as one of unnatural vice brought under such laws, and it may well have been at least partly for this reason that these Gothic princes imported into their statutes the spirit of the Theodosian Code, with the enactments of which against homosexual practices they would be familiar.

There is nothing in the legislation of the Carolingian reform to detain us. Condemnations of homosexual practices in the Capitularies fall roughly into two main groups. Three enactments[4]

---

[1] Doubtless *Lex Visigoth.* III. v. 4.
[2] I.e., 689–690—there is no trace of any canon passed in this year, however, and the reference is probably to *Conc. Toletan. XVI*, 3, the date of which is 693; see above, p. 93.
[3] For the text, see *Mon. Germ. Hist.*, op. cit., p. 165.
[4] *Capit. Carol. mag. et Ludovic. pii*, v. 82 (Mansi, op. cit., xvii b, col. 839); vii. 351 (Mansi, op. cit., xvii b, col. 1101); *Canones Isaac episc. Lingonen.* iv. 11 (Mansi, op. cit., xvii b, col. 1259).

against *eos qui cum . . . masculis contra naturam peccant* borrow their wording from an ordinance of Aix-la-Chapelle in 789 in which appeal is made to the authority of the Latin interpretations of canon 16 of the Council of Ancyra[1]—a canon directed, as we have already seen,[2] against bestiality and not against homosexual acts. Three others simply repeat the prohibition of a capitulary of 803[3] against *sceleres nefandas,* including *sodomitica luxuria*.[4] Finally, a capitulary of Charles the Great condemns sodomy among monks, of which there had been reports, together with other abuses.[5] Much of this legislation thus amounts to nothing more than the routine repetition of existing laws, the terms of one being for the most part automatically reproduced in its successors. A similar pattern of influence can be traced later in the case of a canon of the third Lateran Council (1179) against *incontinentia illa quæ contra naturam est, propter quam venit ira Dei in filios diffidentiæ,*[6] the substance of which, and often its precise wording, is echoed in synodical legislation for the next century.[7]

The most extensive set of enactments against homosexual practices during mediæval times appears in some canons issued by a council held at Naplouse (the ancient Sichem) on 23rd January

---

[1] *Capit. Aquisgran.* 48 (Mansi, op. cit., xvii b, col. 230).

[2] See pp. 86–89.

[3] "*Capit. VIII*", see Mansi, op. cit., xvii b, col. 412.

[4] Capitularies of 814, cap. 2 (Mansi, op. cit., xvii b, col 526); *Capit. Carol. mag. et Ludovic. pii,* vii, 143 (Mansi, op. cit., xvii b, col. 1055); ibid. *additio* ii, 22 (Mansi, op. cit., xvii b, col. 1143).

[5] *Capit. primum Carol. mag.* (802), 17 (Mansi, op. cit., xvii b, col. 368).

[6] *Conc. III Lateran.,* sess. iii. 11 (Mansi, op. cit., xxii, coll. 224–225). There seems to have been some doubt at one time whether this canon did not refer to bestiality, but by the end of the 16th century it was established that it referred to sodomy. It is difficult to imagine how this dubiety arose, in view of the allusion in the canon to the fact that *quinque civitates igne consumpsit.* See R. Brouillard, art. "Bestialité", in *Dictionnaire de Droit Canonique* (Paris, 1924 ff.).

[7] Cf. (a) *Conc. Paris.* (1212), ii. 21 and iii. 2 (Mansi, op. cit., xxii, coll. 831, 834), repeated in *Conc. Rotomag.* (1214), ii. 24 (Mansi, op. cit., xxii, col. 910), and in *Præcept. ant. diœc. Rotomag.* (1235), 40 (Mansi, op. cit., xxiii, col. 379); (b) *Conc. IV Lateran.* (1215), 14 (Mansi, op. cit., xxii, col. 1003), repeated in *Conc. Biterr.* (1246), 19 (Mansi, op. cit., xxiii, col. 696); *Stat. syn. eccl. Cenoman.* (1247), 3 (Mansi, op. cit., xxiii, col. 755); *Stat. syn. eccl. Claromont.* (1268), ii. 1 (Mansi, op. cit., xxiii, col. 1203).

1120 by Baldwin II, king of Jerusalem, and Garmund, patriarch of Jerusalem. Mansi mentions[1] that on this occasion a sermon was preached in which all the ills that had befallen the kingdom of Jerusalem, as well as earthquakes, menacing signs, and the attacks of the Saracens, were attributed to evil living. Thereupon the council proceeded to pass twenty-five canons, mostly directed against sins of the flesh, among which were four aimed specially at sodomists:

CONC. NEAPOLITAN. 8: 'If any adult shall be proved to have defiled himself voluntarily by sodomitical vice, whether actively (*faciens*) or passively (*patiens*), let him be burnt.'

9: 'If a child (*infans*) or anyone else, forcibly compelled by another, shall have been defiled by sodomy, and meanwhile shall have called out loudly,[2] let the sodomist be consigned to the flames, but let him who did not sin willingly do penance according to the rule of the Church, and not be penalized by the law.'

10: 'If anyone who has been forcibly compelled to submit to the crime of sodomy shall conceal the fact and shall allow himself to be polluted again, and shall not make it known to the magistrate, when proof has been secured, let him be judged as a sodomist.'

11: 'If any sodomist, before he is accused, shall come to his senses, and having been brought to penitence, shall renounce that abominable vice by the swearing of an oath, let him be received into the Church and dealt with according to the provisions of the canons. But if he falls a second time into such practices and wishes again to do penance, he may be admitted to penance, but let him be expelled from the kingdom of Jerusalem.'[3]

It is important to bear in mind that these canons were put forth by a mixed assembly of clerics and laymen which had been convened in order to deal with local questions which concerned both Church and State. The constitution and purpose of this council explain the unusual reference to the death penalty. There

---

[1] Op. cit., xxi, coll. 261–262.

[2] If the person assaulted did not call for assistance, it might be assumed (at least in the case of an adult) that he had eventually acquiesced in the act.

[3] See Mansi, op. cit., xxi, col. 264.

is no question of this being imposed by the Church; indeed, all four enactments are really civil in character, and do not attempt to lay down any regulations for dealing with sodomists under ecclesiastical law. They do, however, exempt the penitent offender from the capital sentence and hand him over to the spiritual authority to be put under discipline in accordance with the provisions of the existing canons. Thus they illustrate the co-ordination of the functions of the secular and the religious powers in the administration of the criminal law in connexion with homosexual offences; they reflect the spirit of Justinian's 77th and 141st *novellæ*, and show that some endeavour was being made in judicial practice to express the principle that justice must be tempered with mercy. While the extreme punishment awaited the hardened sodomist, even he might be excused if, before his crime was reported to the magistrate, he came to his senses and submitted to the penitential rules of the Church;[1] and should he lapse and again repent, he might again be admitted to penance— though in such an event the civil authority intervened with a sentence of banishment, so as to prevent the offender from becoming a menace to the community in the future.

With these canons of the Council of Naplouse we may close our survey of the ecclesiastical legislation dealing with homo-sexual practices. Despite its brevity, nothing of importance has been omitted (apart from material which is better considered in connexion with the Penitentials, and one enactment by the Council of London in 1102, to which reference will be made later[2]), and nothing more of note remains to be recorded. Even Gratian, in his *Decretum*, does not discuss the question, and devotes almost no attention to it, but contents himself with setting down without comment three passages, of which the first

---

[1] It is worth nothing that by the end of the 12th century sodomy had become one of the "reserved" sins which had to be referred to high authority—cf. *Synod. Constit. Odo. episc. Paris* (c. 1196), 4, 5 (the Pope, or the bishop); *Conc. Prov. Fritzlar.* (1246), 4 (the bishop or one of his penitentiaries); *Stat. syn. eccl. Leod.* (1287), iv. 11 (the bishop); *Conc. Remense* (1408): see Mansi, op. cit., xxiii, col. 678; xxiii, col. 726; xxiv. col. 891; xxvi, col. 1073.

[2] See p. 124.

H

two are simply steps in an argument concerned with the different species of fornication. One, from Augustine's *Confessions*,[1] we have already met:[2] '. . . those shameful acts against nature, such as were committed in Sodom, ought everywhere and always to be detested and punished . . .';[3] the second, from a pseudo-Augustinian treatise *Contra Jovinianum*, insists that the use against nature is always unlawful, and without doubt more shameful and filthy than fornication and adultery;[4] and the third merely repeats the opinion of the jurist Paulus[5] concerning *stuprum pueri*.[6] These passages add nothing to our knowledge of the Church's attitude to homosexual practices; while the *Extravagantes* of Pope Gregory IX, a supplementary collection of canons and material from decretals, only reproduces the canons of the third and fourth Lateran Councils against sodomy.[7]

From an examination of this somewhat meagre body of legislation no particular trend or pattern emerges, and no features stand out with any special prominence. Such development or change as we find is no more than we would expect to find. Just as Church Orders and early canons insist upon the rejection of sodomists from the catechumenate, so this rule disappears with the virtual desuetude of adult initiation. From time to time councils and synods denounce sodomy no less than other grave carnal sins—and occasionally the godly prince finds that the claims of morality and the promptings of superstition have their political convenience; yet we look in vain for that obsessive concern with this one offence which many have imagined that they have detected in the records of ecclesiastical legislation. Indeed, it is striking to observe how relatively small a place in conciliar and synodal proceedings is occupied by condemnations of homosexual practices. This does not imply of course, that such practices were either comparatively rare, or regarded with complacency—and they are often denounced (though not actually

---

[1] Conf. III. viii [15].   [2] See p. 83.
[3] C. XXXII, q. vii, c. 13.   [4] C. XXXII, q. vii, c. 14.
[5] *Sent.* V. iv. 14 = *Dig.* XLVII. xi. 1, § 2.; see p. 68.
[6] *De pœnit.*, d. I, c. xv.   [7] See X. V. xxxi, 4 and X. III. i. 13.

specified) in many general enactments against the sins of the flesh, and especially those regarded as contrary to nature. But it does give the lie to a common accusation made against the Church; some one hundred items of legislation at most (several of these enacted by the same council, and many more borrowed from a single source and repeated) during a period of more than a thousand years is hardly convincing proof of an implacable ecclesiastical animus against the sodomist. He is certainly denounced as one guilty of very grave sin, but he is not singled out for any sadistic persecution; he is offered reconciliation with God and man through the Church's penitential discipline, but if he refuses the means of grace, he has to take the eternal consequences of his sin and the temporal consequences of his crime—and both Church and State deal with him according to contemporary notions of morality and punishment.

Nor was sodomy, as it has recently been said, 'above all the failing of the priesthood, as one can tell from the numerous church edicts on the subject'.[1] Of the canons and other ordinances against homosexual acts, only a small proportion are directed against monks or clerics—usually in special circumstances, as in the case of 'a church council' of 1102 to which the writer refers.[2] True, the Penitentials deal fully with homosexual practices of many kinds by priests and monastics, but this is explained by the purpose of these handbooks;[3] there is no reliable evidence that all the sins detailed in their pages were actually—let alone habitually—committed. They were included in order to afford guidance to the confessor, should he ever need to appoint the appropriate penance. No doubt, as Basil and Augustine realized, special temptations attended the life of a monk, but there is no reason to suppose that the Penitentials reflect the normal life of a well-governed monastery any more than do the calumnies broadcast later by some of the racier propagandists among the reformers. If the failings of the mediæval priesthood in particular are to be

---

[1] G. Rattray Taylor, *Sex in History* (London, 1953), p. 34.
[2] See below, pp. 124–125.
[3] See below, p. 100.

assessed statistically on the basis of ecclesiastical legislation, contravention of the rule of clerical celibacy would appear to have been a far more typical lapse than homosexual indulgences.

3. THE PENITENTIALS

The Penitentials originated in the Celtic Churches of Ireland and Wales, whence their use and influence spread to England, France, Germany, and even Italy; thus, in spite of manifest defects, they affected a very considerable proportion of Western Christendom, and determined for some five centuries the standards according to which penance was administered. Here we are not concerned with the question of the Penitentials in general;[1] they are important for the present study because they illustrate more fully than the enactments of councils and synods how the Church attempted to deal with homosexual offenders, and to discriminate as fairly as possible between different kinds of acts according to their nature and circumstances. The value of the Penitentials, however, is limited by their formalism and their lack of system and uniformity, and in particular (for our purpose) by the absence of any rationale of the principles according to which sexual acts are distinguished as more or less sinful.

It is necessary first to make clear the purpose of the Penitentials. They were first and foremost simply manuals for confessors, designed to give guidance in the administration of private penance, and their comprehensiveness is due to the fact that they provide lists of sins which were no doubt intended to be read out to the penitent to put him in mind of his trespasses. These catalogues do not imply that any of the sins detailed were common, though the compilers were probably helped by a fairly intimate knowledge of the lives and conduct of the people among whom the priest would be called to minister. In particular, there is no indication of any obsession with sexual offences, though it has sometimes been alleged that they are treated at undue length.

---

[1] For a good general introduction to the Penitentials, see R. C. Mortimer, *Western Canon Law* (London, 1953), pp. 24 ff.

Thus Mr. G. Rattray Taylor states that 'The penitentials . . .
devoted a disproportionately large amount of their space to
prescribing penalties for homosexuality and for bestiality',[1] but
an examination of the three English Penitentials of Theodore,
Bede, and Ecgbert does not bear out this assertion; it shows that
of the total number of clauses in each, only 3·5 per cent, 8 per cent,
and 5·5 per cent respectively are concerned with homosexual
practices—and in the case of bestiality the proportions are much
smaller. While these figures do not suggest any disproportionate
attention to homosexual offences, they certainly indicate a laudable
desire to discriminate between different kinds of acts in order to
fit the penance equitably to the sin—a point which is often overlooked.

To give anything like a reasonably complete synopsis of the
provisions relating to homosexual practices in the various
Penitentials would prove a large and complicated task; fortu-
nately, however, a select but adequate account is possible without
entering into what would inevitably be tediously repetitive
detail. Confining our attention, therefore, to twelve Penitentials
of differing date and provenance,[2] we may first notice how
homosexual acts are distinguished according to their nature and

---

[1] Op. cit., p. 54.

[2] The following are the documents from which material has been drawn; the
symbol in square brackets after each is that by means of which reference will be
made to it in this section:

   (i) The canons of the Synod of Llanddewi-Brefi [L–B]—ante 569.
   (ii) The canons of the Synod of *Lucus Victoriæ* [L–V]—569.
   (iii) Gildas: *Præfatio de Penitentia* [G]—ante 570.
   (iv) *Liber S. David.* [D]—6th cent.
   (v) The Penitential of Columban [Col.]—c. 600.
   (vi) The Penitential of Cummean [Cum.]—7th cent.
   (vii) Theodore's Penitential [T]—c. 670.
   (viii) Bede's Penitential [B]—ante 734.
   (ix) Ecgbert's Penitential [E]—? 732–766.
   (x) *Pænitentiale Burgundense* [Burg.]—c. 700–725.
   (xi) *Pænitentiale Romanum* (so-called) of Halitgar [R]—c. 830.
   (xii) The Penitential of Thorlac Thorhallson (Iceland) [T–T]—c. 1008–1012.

Nos. i–iv are British or Irish; nos. v, vi, x, and xi, Frankish; and nos. vii–ix,
Anglo-Saxon.

circumstances. Thus, varying penances are assigned (in ascending order of severity) for kissing, licentious kissing, and kissing with accompanying emission, between boys under twenty years of age; for kissing between young men over twenty; for mutual masturbation, inter-femoral connexion, and "fornication" (not more exactly specified); and finally for *fellatio* and sodomy proper.[1] Some Penitentials discriminate between those who adopt the passive and the active roles,[2] between occasional and habitual indulgence,[3] and between first and subsequent offences.[4] Distinctions are also drawn between the classes of person who may commit homosexual acts; monks are to be dealt with differently from laymen,[5] boys and youths from older men,[6] and the various grades of the ministry one from another.[7] Provision is also made for special cases, such as a brother fornicating with his natural brother (a sort of homosexual "incest"),[8] one lay woman indulging in homosexual acts with another,[9] and nuns using an artificial phallus ([*fornicantes*] *per machinam*).[10]

Generally speaking, clergymen in higher orders are penalized more heavily than those in lower orders, monks and priests more heavily than the laity, and men more heavily than boys, youths, or women—nuns, in the case of the last, being treated more severely than lay women. Thus in dealing with sodomy, Ecgbert's

---

[1] The most comprehensive range of distinctions between homosexual acts is to be found in Cum. (ii. 8, 9, 10; x. 2, 3, 6, 7, 8, 9, 14, 16) and R (6, 13, and 67); T distinguishes between inter-femoral connexion (I. ii. 8; viii. 10), sodomy (I. ii. 6, 7), *fellatio* (I. ii. 15—not I. vii. 3, which refers to drinking blood or semen for magical purposes), and various kinds of homosexual fornication (I. ii, 2, 4, 5, 11, 19); and L–V (viii) and B (iii. 19, 20, 21, 22, 30, 31, 32) between mutual masturbation, inter-femoral connexion, and sodomy.

[2] Cum. (x. 9); T (I. ii. 6); E (v. 17).

[3] Cum. (ii. 8; x. 7, 8, 16); T (I. ii. 7); B (iii. 20); E (v. 17).

[4] Cum. (x. 14); T (I. ii. 7); E. (v. 18).

[5] Col. (3, 15); E. (i, ii. 2—cf. v. 17); R (13).

[6] Cum. (x. 2, 3, 6, 9); T (I. ii. 4, 5, 11); B (iii. 21, 22, 30, 31, 32).

[7] E (i, ii. 2).

[8] T (I. ii. 19); E (iv. 5).   [9] T (I. ii. 12); B (iii. 23).

[10] B (iii. 24); cf. *Libri Reginonis de eccl. discipl.*, ii, 250, in B. Thorpe, *The Ancient Laws and Institutes of England* (London, 1840), ii, p. 83: *Si sanctimonialis cum alia sanctimoniali per aliquod machinamentum fornicatur . . .*

Penitential imposes a penance of at least five years on a cleric, as compared with a minimum of four years for a layman,[1] while Halitgar's *Pœnitentiale Romanum* gives ten years and seven years respectively.[2] For inter-femoral connexion, Theodore's Penitential requires a cleric to do penance for three years, but stipulates only one year, or alternatively three forty-day periods, for a layman.[3]

Comparing the penances assigned to boys and youths with those assigned to men, we find that for inter-femoral connexion Cummean's Penitential prescribes a penance of two years for men, of one year for youths over twenty, and of one hundred days for boys under that age,[4] while Bede's Penitential penalizes men and youths over twenty with three forty-day periods of penance, and boys under twenty with a penance of one hundred days.[5] Similarly, in the case of acts between older and younger boys or youths (presumably resident in the monasteries) a distinction is made. Boys under twenty who indulge in kissing are given a penance of six special fasts by Cummean's Penitential; if the kissing is licentious the penance is increased to eight special fasts, and if it is accompanied by emission or embraces,[6] to ten;[7] but if youths over twenty kiss, they are required to live in continence, and to sit at separate tables for meals, eating only bread and drinking water, and are excluded from the church.[8] A small boy engaging in passive sodomy (presumably with an adult) is compelled by Bede's Penitential to do penance for forty days; but if a boy acts thus, even voluntarily, with an older boy, his penance is only one of twenty days.[9] Women who indulge in lesbianism are assigned a penance of three years,[10] but nuns receive seven years.[11]

Many illustrations could be given of the lack of uniformity and system in the Penitentials. When different penances are laid down

---

[1] E (i).   [2] R (6, 13).
[3] T (I. ii. 8; viii. 10).   [4] Cum. (ii. 10; x. 8).
[5] B (iii. 21, 31).
[6] Presumably this means attempted connexion of some kind.
[7] Cum. (x. 2).
[8] Cum. (x. 3); the period of penance is not stated, and presumably lay in the discretion of the confessor.
[9] B (iii. 22, 32).   [10] T (I. ii. 12); B (iii. 23).   [11] B (iii. 24).

for the same sin in the same code, it is often because the compiler has assembled the divergent views or practices of several authorities, thus leaving the confessor a certain latitude in his administration of discipline. On the other hand, variations may be due to the fact that on different occasions the same authority (for example, Archbishop Theodore of Canterbury, very many of whose decisions are undoubtedly incorporated in the code which bears his name) prescribed different penances for the same offence (or was supposed to have done) all of which were eventually recorded indiscriminately and without comment.

Consider, for instance, the treatment of sodomy in Ecgbert's Penitential. First, sodomy practised habitually (*in consuetudine*) is numbered among the *capitalia crimina* for which the following periods of penance are assigned: layman, four years; *clericus,* five years; subdeacon, six years; deacon, seven years; priest, ten years; and bishop, twelve years.[1] In the next chapter, however, we find habitual sodomy included with theft, false witness, and fornication, among the *minora peccata,*[2] although the penances, curiously enough, are more severe: layman, five years; *clericus,* seven years; subdeacon, eight years; deacon, ten years; priest twelve years; bishop, fourteen years.[3] Finally, in the chapter *De Clericorum Penitentia,* the following clause appears:[4]

> 'If a man commits sodomy often, or if one doing so is in orders, some hold that he must do penance for ten years; others say, for seven years; others again, for one year if he has taken the passive role (*molles*); others, for one hundred days, if the offender is a boy.'

With these provisions may be compared those in the Collection of Regino of Prum:[5]

> 'Some consider that he who commits fornication like a sodomist must do penance for ten years; others, for seven years; others again,

---

[1] E (i).
[2] In one MS. of this Penitential (Bodl. 718), however, there is a separate chapter, *De Sodomitis,* under which these penances are detailed.
[3] E (ii. 2).   [4] E (v. 17).
[5] *Lib. Reg. de eccl. discipl.,* ii. 254; see B. Thorpe, op. cit., ii, p. 84.

for one year. Some hold that if the practice is habitual, a layman must do five years penance; a *clericus*, seven years; one who is a sub-deacon or a monk, eight years; a deacon, ten years; a priest, twelve years; and a bishop, thirteen years.'

Similar variations exist in regard to other offences. Theodore's Penitential reports a diversity of opinion as to the penance to be applied in cases of *fellatio*; some say that he who commits this *pessimum malum* must do penance for seven years, others say, for twenty-two years, and yet others, for life.[1] Nor is consistency as between the different codes to be expected when internal uni-formity is absent. In earlier Penitentials the penance for sodomy is three[2] or four[3] years, while the *Liber S. David.* simply says: 'Dead to the world, let them live unto God'.[4] Later, as more and more categories of penitent are included, the penances become more severe, and their range increases. One Penitential stipulates that the period for sodomists is from four to seven years, according to the circumstances of the offence;[5] another requires seven years,[6] and a third, from seven to ten years;[7] others again impose periods of nine or ten years,[8] ten years,[9] from one to fourteen years,[10] and from two to fifteen years.[11]

It is interesting to compare these penances with those allocated to other sins. Taking a fairly comprehensive Penitential, that of Theodore, we find that the following terms of discipline were assigned, having regard to the circumstances and the persons concerned: for homosexual "fornication" (unspecified), from ten to fifteen years; for sodomy, from seven to fifteen years; for *fellatio*, from seven years (but it is unlikely that the excessive terms of twenty-two years or life were normally imposed); for lesbianism, three years; and for inter-femoral connexion, a

---

[1] T (I. ii. 15).
[2] L–B (i)—with expulsion to another monastery; G (i and ii).
[3] L–V (viii).   [4] D (v).
[5] B (iii. 19, 20).   [6] Cum. (ii. 9).
[7] Col. (*Capital Offences*, 3, 15; *Monks*, 3); R (6, 13).
[8] T–T.
[9] Burg. (4).
[10] E (i, ii. 2, v. 17).   [11] T (I. ii. 6–7).

maximum of one year.[1] The same Penitential (to mention a few items) stipulated fifteen years penance for incest and heterosexual fornication,[2] and for infanticide[3] (this was reduced to seven years if the woman was a pauper[4]); eleven years for perjury committed in church;[5] from seven to ten years for homicide;[6] and seven years for adultery by a wife,[7] or for persistent theft.[8] A man who divorced his wife and remarried had to do seven years penance *cum tribulatione*; otherwise the period was extended to fifteen years.[9] Although homosexual offences are by no means treated leniently in this code, it is evident by comparison with the penances set for other sins that no unduly harsh discrimination is to be exercised against those who own themselves guilty of homosexual practices. A penitential regulation of Pope Gregory III (731–741) well expresses both the general Christian attitude at the time towards such acts, and the desire of those responsible for the Church's discipline that penances should be at once equitable and proportionate to the gravity (as it was thought) of the offence:

JUDICIA GREG. PAP. III, 21: 'If any ordained person has been defiled with the crime of sodomy, which is described as a vice so abominable in the sight of God that the cities in which its practitioners dwelt were appointed for destruction by fire and brimstone, let him do penance for ten years, according to the ancient rule. Some, however, being more humanely disposed, have fixed the term at seven years. Those also who are ignorant of the gravity of this offence are assigned three years in which to do penance. As for boys who know that they are indulging in this practice, it behoves them to hasten to amend; let them do penance for fifty days, and in addition let them be beaten with rods; for it is necessary that the crop which has brought forth bad fruit be cut down.'[10]

---

[1] References for these penances have already been given above.
[2] I. ii. 16, 17.   [3] I. xiv. 25.
[4] I. xiv. 26.   [5] I. vi. 1.
[6] I. iv. 1, 3.   [7] I. xiv. 14.
[8] I. iii. 1.
[9] I. xiv. 8.
[10] See Mansi, op. cit., xii, col. 293. In § 30 (ibid., col. 295) we read: . . . *Si qua mulier cum altera coitum fecerit quatuor quadragesimas pœniteat . . .*

So far we have not considered the full provisions of any one Penitential for dealing with homosexual offences. There is no particular pattern to which even the main codes conform, and inclusions and omissions seem to have been dictated by the choice of the compiler—and possibly owe not a little to the precedents upon which he was able to draw. Some Penitentials contain very little material bearing upon our study, while others are elaborate and detailed in their rules; but as a fair specimen we may, in conclusion, set out the penances assigned to homosexual acts by the Penitential of Cummean—bearing in mind that these would form but a small proportion of the total number of sins of all kinds treated in such a code.

THE PENITENTIAL OF CUMMEAN

1. Kissing:
   (a) If under twenty years of age (x. 2):
      (i) Simple kissing: to be corrected with six special fasts;
      (ii) Licentiously, but without emission: eight special fasts.
      (iii) With emission or embrace: ten special fasts.
   (b) If over twenty years of age: to live in continence, at separate tables, on bread and water, and to be excluded from church (x. 3).

2. Mutual masturbation by those over twenty years of age:
   (a) If the practice is confessed: to do penance for twenty or forty days before receiving the Communion (x. 6).
   (b) If repeated after penance has been done: a further penance of one hundred days; if frequently repeated: the persons concerned are to be separated, and to do penance for a year (x. 7).

3. Inter-femoral connexion:
   (a) A penance of two years (ii. 10); or
   (b) A penance of one hundred days for the first offence, and of one year for the second (x. 8).

4. *Fellatio* (ii. 8; x. 16):

   (a) A penance of four years.

   (b) If habitual, a penance of seven years.

5. Sodomy: a penance of seven years (ii. 9).

6. If a small boy under the age of ten is abused by an older boy, he must fast for a week (x. 9).

7. Homosexual practices (unspecified)—(x. 14):

   (a) For a first offence: a penance of one year.

   (b) If repeated: a penance of two years.

It will be noticed that there is no attempt made here to discriminate between penitents, except on the score of age, and that clergy and laity are treated alike; also, that no mention is made of lesbianism, and no distinction is drawn between active and passive sodomy, or between occasional and habitual indulgence in this practice. All these features are to be found, as we have seen, in one or other of the remaining Penitentials; but these, on the other hand (with the exception of Halitgar's *Pœnitentiale Romanum*), do not deal with kissing. Thus the scope and the limitations of the individual Penitentials are effectively illustrated.

Surveying the Penitentials as a whole, and comparing them with the ecclesiastical opinion and legislation already described, their most striking feature is undoubtedly seen to be the recognition that homosexual acts between men commonly take various forms, of which sodomy proper is only one—a distinction virtually ignored hitherto. Not all such acts are regarded as equally culpable, particularly when committed by boys or youths, and clerics and monks are expected, apparently, to conform to a higher moral standard than that required of the laity; nevertheless all homosexual practices are held to be sinful in some measure, and certain acts are regarded as transgressions of special gravity. The fact that sodomy (which probably meant other kinds of homosexual act as well) was eventually treated as a sin to be reserved for reference to the pope, or to the bishop and his penitentiaries,[1] suggests that confessors did not always succeed in exercising the discretion and judgement required by the Penitentials when alternative impositions were provided or considerable latitude was allowed.

It may, of course, be contended that such detailed discrimination between the various homosexual acts was unnecessary—and we have seen that this has sometimes been misinterpreted as evidence of early mediæval licentiousness or prurient obsession with the subject. But it is surely in fact not open to dispute that, given the system implied by the Penitentials—a system excellent in purpose if not always in its operation—the administration of the Church's discipline demanded that such guidance should be afforded to the confessor to enable him to exercise his office efficiently and fairly. On one point, however, information would be invaluable. We do not know the principles (or perhaps better, the nexus of religious conviction, prejudice, and superstition) which determined the scaling of penances; and although in many cases a guess can be made with some considerable degree of probability, it cannot be checked against any contemporary rationale of the Christian attitude to homosexual practices. Later, as we shall see, attempts at explanation are made.

One significant feature must not be overlooked; in several codes we find for the first time that lesbianism is recognized and penalized—though as we would expect, less heavily than sodomy. Yet while mention is made of the use (only by nuns) of what can only be the artificial phallus, female homosexual practices are not otherwise differentiated.

Finally, in considering the penances assigned to homosexual as well as to other offences by the Penitentials, it is important to remember that it eventually became possible to secure some mitigation of their severity by means of a system of commutations. It would not be untrue to say that these codes were penal rather than genuinely penitential in spirit, and tended to emphasize the payment of satisfaction for the sins committed rather than the

---

[1] See above, p. 97.

arousal of contrition and a desire for amendment of life. For instance, the fact that a penance of seven years was imposed for sodomy meant that this was the period of punishment regarded as appropriate to the crime, and sufficient to secure the deliverance of the sinner from the torments of hell. But so long as the quantitative obligation of the penance was duly discharged, the method was of secondary importance—just as it is immaterial to the law whether a fine is paid by the person convicted, or by someone else on his behalf. A period of discipline, therefore, might be shortened by ascetic exercises of exceptional rigour, or even reduced by vicarious means.[1] Thus it should not be assumed that the penances allocated by the Penitentials to homosexual offences were always and necessarily performed in full; no doubt, as with other sins, the satisfaction required was often discharged with the minimum of inconvenience by means of recourse to commutation or the kind offices of friends.

4. MEDIÆVAL OPINION AND TEACHING

It is always difficult to know how accurately an item of synodical legislation, a penitential, or the writing of this or that theologian reflects either the contemporary prevalence of homosexual practices or the current opinion concerning them—just as it is uncertain today how much reliance can be placed upon press reports or police statistics as indications of the state of sexual morality in the community. We have no concrete and independent evidence, for instance, by means of which to assess the allegations of Boniface and five German bishops in a letter to King Ethelbald of Mercia (c. 744–747) that '. . . the people of England (as it has been spread abroad throughout these provinces and is held to our reproach in France and Italy—and is regarded by the pagans themselves as improper) have been living a shameful life, despising lawful marriages, committing adultery, and lusting after the fashion of the people of Sodom. . . .'[2] Does this imply a

---

[1] For examples, see R. C. Mortimer, op. cit, pp. 29–31.

[2] For the text, see Haddan and Stubbs, op. cit., iii, p. 354; cf. the letter written at the same time by Boniface to Archbishop Ecgbert of York, ibid., iii, p. 359.

notable increase in sexual vice, including sodomy, or are these simply the typical assertions of the outraged moralist and reformer as he contemplates what appears to him to be the unprecedented corruption of his time?

Such questions are inevitably prompted by what is in some respects the most notable mediæval pronouncement upon the subject of homosexual practices—the *Liber Gomorrhianus* of Peter Damiani (1007–1072). This extraordinary composition, published about the year 1051, seems to have been occasioned by the author's alarm at the spread of such practices among the clergy, particularly in his own neighbourhood—he was at that time head of the monastery of Fonte Avellana, near Gubbio. He conceived it to be his duty to call the attention of Pope Leo IX to the existence of this scandal, and to discuss for his benefit the different kinds of *peccatum contra naturam* and the appropriate methods of dealing with those who indulged in them. To this task he brought the same energy, vehemence of style, and vigour of invective which had already characterized his polemic against the concubinage and marriage of priests, and which fully justifies the description of him by Bernard of Constance as "the Jerome of our times". The result was a treatise which has considerable interest as the record of an attitude to homosexual practices no less common at the present than in the past, though its historical value as evidence of the extent of these practices and of the general ecclesiastical opinion regarding them is much less certain.

Peter recognizes only three varieties of homosexual act practised by males[1]—mutual masturbation, inter-femoral connexion, and sodomy, in ascending order of gravity;[2] these, he holds, should be penalized in proportion to the seriousness of each offence—but not even for the first has he anything but the harshest censure.[3] Indeed, he declares that in his opinion bestiality

---

[1] Female homosexual practices are not mentioned.

[2] In addition to homosexual practices, he also deals with solitary masturbation, which was always classed among the *peccata contra naturam*, though regarded less seriously than the others named.

[3] *Lib. Gomorrh.* 1 (see Migne, *Patrologia Latina*, cxlv, col. 161).

is less grave a crime than homosexual lust: *ut mihi videtur, tolerabilius est cum pecude quam cum viro in luxuriæ flagitium labi;*[1] and he expresses himself with special force on the subject of acts committed by *spirituales patres* with their *spirituales filii*[2]—though it is not certain whether he means by these terms confessors with penitents, or sponsors with godsons. He laments over the fate of the souls of those who abandon themselves to practices so foul that they are unknown among animals.[3] What does a man seek in another man? he asks; What can he hope to find that is not already in himself?[4] Such conduct is particularly heinous in a priest, for God will not accept any sacrifice from hands stained by filthy acts,[5] nor any oblation of sanctity which has been defiled by pollution.[6]

Some of Peter Damiani's most contemptuous denunciations are reserved for the Penitentials and their method of assigning what were, to him, wholly inadequate punishments for homosexual offences. Who invented these codes and their schemes of penance? he demands; Who sowed such sharp, prickly thistles in the Church's fair groves? Some say of a rule that it originated with Theodore; others, that it is to be found in the *Pœnitentiale Romanum*, or in the Canons of the Apostles—but what authority can the contents of these manuals possess, when their authors are unknown or in dispute? Yet against all such *scenica deliramenta* (as he calls them) he sets 'those canons, the reliability and weight of which we have absolutely no reason to distrust as uncertain'— and these prove to be the sixteenth and seventeenth of the Council of Ancyra, which originally had (as we have seen) no reference to sodomy, but acquired a homosexual significance

---

1 *Lib. Gomorrh.* 6 (Migne, *P.L.*, cxlv, col. 167).
2 Ibid., 6, 8, 9 (Migne, *P.L.*, cxlv, coll. 166, 168–169).
3 Ibid., 17 (Migne, *P.L.*, cxlv, col. 177). The assumption that homosexual practices are unknown among animals we now know to be unfounded, for a considerable volume of evidence has been collected regarding the sexual habits of beasts and birds which disproves it; see e.g., Ellis, op. cit., ii, pp. 4–8.
4 *Lib. Gomorrh.* 17 (Migne, *P.L.*, cxlv, col. 178).
5 Ibid., 20 (Migne, *P.L.*, cxlv, col. 181).
6 Ibid., 21 (Migne, *P.L.*, cxlv, col. 182).

through the erroneous Latin *Interpretationes!*[1] Elsewhere, however,[2] he quotes Basil's directions concerning the discipline of sodomists.

No objection is proof against Peter's arguments. If a man has inter-femoral connexion with another man, it is clear that he ought to do penance, but surely (it might be urged) humanity forbids his being irrevocably degraded from his order? Peter brushes this plea aside: it is self-evident, he says, that he who does this with a man would rather, if nature had made it possible, use the male as a female; since, however, this cannot be (for anatomical reasons), he does what he can—but ought he not to be treated in the same way as one who violates a virgin, for his offence is comparable in purpose?[3] Every kind of *peccatum contra naturam* deserves the maximum penalty, without admitting the least mitigation: we do not read that the Sodomites committed nothing but sodomy; on the contrary we must believe that, impelled by the frenzy of lust, they performed all sorts of vile acts upon themselves or upon others![4] Hence those in authority are wrong who have ordered that no one is to be degraded from his order because he has committed offences other than sodomy.[5]

One practice against which Peter protests is that of homosexual offenders confessing to the persons with whom the acts in question were committed, thus ensuring that the matter would go no further, and that the penance would probably be trivial. Of what avail were such confessions? The leper ought to show himself to the priest, and not to another leper; how can a confessor who is himself bound exercise his power of binding and loosing?[6]

No sooner did this treatise appear than it aroused a storm of indignant protest. Some, accused perhaps by their consciences, were furious at its publication and resented the imputations made

---

[1] *Lib. Gomorrh.* 10, 11, 12 (Migne, *P.L.*, cxlv, coll. 169–172).
[2] Ibid., 15 (Migne, *P.L.*, cxlv, col. 174).
[3] Ibid., 8 (Migne, *P.L.*, cxlv, col. 168).
[4] Ibid., 22 (Migne, *P.L.*, cxlv, col. 183).
[5] Ibid., 2 (Migne, *P.L.*, cxlv, col. 162).
[6] Ibid., 7 (Migne, *P.L.*, cxlv, col. 167).

against certain of the clergy; others feared that such a bold exposure of vice might do more harm than good, and that the very force of Peter's attack would only encourage exaggerated ideas as to the extent of the evil.[1] Leo IX himself, though he had at first welcomed and approved the *Liber Gomorrhianus* and had accepted the author's dedication,[2] now began to have second thoughts. Further reflection upon the contents and style of the book, aided no doubt by the strictures of the critics, convinced him that Peter had gone too far, and he felt bound to administer a check to the reformer's intemperate zeal.

After commending, therefore, the motive behind his courageous and forthright defence of chastity and condemnation of clerical vice, the pope went on to rebuke his harsh and unyielding spirit. Leo agreed that all homosexual acts were not equally sinful and did not merit the same ecclesiastical censure, and that some distinction ought therefore to be made between them in assigning penances; but he could not assent to Peter's drastic proposals for discipline, which generally included the degradation of culprits from their order. *Nos humanius agentes,* he declares, he would not himself go even as far as the canons and strict justice might seem to require in dealing with certain offenders. Those who had indulged in mutual masturbation or in inter-femoral connexion, but not promiscuously or for any length of time, and who had subsequently expiated their sin by an appropriate penance, should be allowed to remain in their order; only those whose practices were of long duration, who had been with many men, or who, *quod horrendum est dictu et auditu,* had actually engaged in sodomy, ought to be punished by deposition. 'And if anyone', the pope concluded, 'should dare to criticize or carp at this decree of ours . . . let him know that *he* is in danger of his order'.[3]

Somewhat mortified by this rebuff, Peter defended himself in a vigorous letter of protest,[4] but apparently without much success,

---

[1] See K. H. Mann, *The Lives of the Popes in the Middle Ages,* iv (London, 1925), p. 52.
[2] Ibid., iv, p. 51.
[3] For the text of Leo's letter, see Mansi, op. cit., xix, coll. 685–686.
[4] See Migne, *Patr. Lat.,* cxliv, coll. 208–209.

and nothing more was heard of the matter. We do not know whether the *Liber Gomorrhianus* effected any marked reformation in clerical morals; to make any assessment of its influence it would first have to be established that homosexual practices by priests and monks abounded on the scale alleged by Peter (and that, more than locally), and of such extensive moral corruption there is no evidence—none, certainly, that would warrant the inference that a wave of sexual perversion was sweeping through the Western Church. Reviewing the affair as a whole and in the light of the chief protagonist's character and views, it seems reasonable to conclude that his onslaught was probably provoked less by an outbreak of vice than by his revulsion from the conduct of a few licentious individuals which had come to his notice, and which served to sharpen the edge of his indignation. The pope's temperate and judicious reply suggests that whatever abuses may have existed, they had greatly been magnified by Peter, and the letter is chiefly remarkable for its emphasis upon the need for a sense of proportion and a humane approach to the question of homosexual practices. In this respect it is a document more valuable, if less curious and arresting, than the *Liber Gomorrhianus*. Leo does not doubt that such acts are indeed *peccata contra naturam* and therefore sinful, and that if habitual and promiscuous they demand severe treatment, while sodomy is specially to be condemned; yet he realizes that the fierce tirades of Peter Damiani are likely to fail in their purpose because of their exaggerated vehemence, and that the heavy penalties demanded by the latter fail to exhibit the Church as the dispenser of God's mercy as well as his judgement, and may hinder it in its task of bringing transgressors to repentance and amendment.

From the *Liber Gomorrhianus* it is a relief to turn to the careful and dispassionate treatment of homosexual practices by Thomas Aquinas, the only great scholastic theologian to discuss the subject in any detail. He deals with it in the *Summa Theologica,* in the course of the treatise on the cardinal virtue of temperance, and develops his argument on the lines following.

One of the vices contrary to temperance is lust, the essence of which is that it 'exceeds the order and mode of reason where venereal acts are concerned'.[1] Discordance with right reason is evident whenever something is done which is inconsistent with the proper end of such acts—and this, it was held universally, is first of all the generation and education of children. Since the *peccatum contra naturam* in any form is directed solely to the pursuit of venereal pleasure and excludes procreation, it clearly offends against reason and falls, therefore, to be considered as one of the species of lust.[2]

This particular vice, however, has one feature which distinguishes it from other lustful venereal acts. Not only, like them, is it contrary to right reason, but it is also 'contrary to the natural order of the venereal act as becoming to the human race.'[3] Hence it is appropriately termed the *vitium contra naturam*, and can occur in four ways: by procuring ejaculation (*pollutio*) without coitus, or masturbation; by copulation with non-human creatures, or bestiality; by *concubitus ad non debitum sexum*—that is, presumably, by coital or other venereal acts performed with one of the same sex;[4] and by deviation from the 'natural manner of [heterosexual] coitus (*naturalis modus concumbendi*)'. It will be seen that these various infringements of the *ordo naturalis venerei actus* do, in fact, cover all forms of male and female homosexual practice, either by definition or by implication—though it is not always easy to determine in which of these four categories each specific act should be placed.

Of the different *peccata contra naturam*, bestiality is stated to be the most grievous; next comes sodomy and after that, non-observance of the *debitus modus concumbendi*, while masturbation is regarded as the least serious, consisting as it does in the mere omission of copulation.[5] Thus it will be seen that as far as homosexual acts are concerned, Aquinas's gradation of offences corresponds roughly to the order of gravity in which such offences are

---

[1] *Summa Theol.*, II–II, Q. cliii, 3; cf. Q. cliii, 2; Q. cliv, 1.
[2] Ibid., II–II, Q. cliv, 1.   [3] Ibid., II–II, Q. cliv, 11.
[4] Both males with males, and females with females, are specified.
[5] *Summa Theol.*, II–II Q. cliv, 12 *ad.* 4.

arranged by the Penitentials, and by both Peter Damiani and Leo IX. It is not clear, however, in what category he would have placed acts such as mutual masturbation or homosexual *fellatio*, which could be regarded either as means of seeking venereal pleasure by causing ejaculation without coitus, or as modes of *concubitus ad non debitum sexum*. But one thing at least is indisputable: even the least serious of these *peccata* is more sinful of its kind than any other species of lust—and in this connexion Aquinas refutes an argument which is often used in defence of homosexual practices.

One objection advanced against the proposition that unnatural vice is the most sinful kind of lust runs as follows: '. . . the more contrary any sin is to charity, the graver is that sin. Now adultery, seduction, and rape, which injure one's neighbour, seem to be more contrary to charity than sins against nature, by which no one else is injured. Therefore the *peccatum contra naturam* is not the greatest among the different kinds of lust'.[1] Against this, however, Aquinas contends that since the order of nature derives from God himself, its contravention is always an injury done to the Creator, whether or not any offence is at the same time committed against one's neighbour. He would hold, therefore, that even homosexual practices between consenting adults, which harm no one (so it would be said), are nevertheless transgressions of the Divine law by which Man's sexual nature is governed.[2]

Another point of interest in this connexion concerns those homosexual acts which might appear to be innocent in themselves, such as touches, caresses, and kisses—it will be recalled that the latter were penalized by certain Penitentials. Aquinas observes that since such acts can be done without lustful pleasure, they are not in themselves mortally sinful, but become so by reason of their motive (*causa*). Consequently, when they are done for the purpose of enjoying forbidden pleasure they are lustful and therefore gravely sinful, for consent to the pleasure of a lustful act is no less sinful than consent to the act itself.[3] Thus indulgence

---

[1] *Summa Theol.*, II–II, Q. cliv, 12, 1.   [2] Ibid., II–II, Q. cliv, 12 *ad*. 1.
[3] Ibid., II–II, Q. cliv, 4.

in homosexual caresses and kisses for the purpose of venereal pleasure is condemned, even when they do not lead to the commission of specific acts; but Aquinas would apparently not consider lustful those acts which are simply expressions of regard or affection between persons of the same sex, provided they are not liable to arouse venereal excitement.

The Church had traditionally condemned homosexual practices as "Sodomitical" and as unnatural; for the first of these grounds Scripture itself was held to afford ample warrant, while for the second Aquinas elaborated a rational and logical proof. Starting from the universally accepted premise that the primary purpose of the sexual organs is procreation—from which it followed that they may only be used legitimately for such acts as do not exclude the possibility (though they may not express the intention) of generation—he found no difficulty in showing that all homosexual practices are *ex hypothesi* unnatural, lustful, and sinful. Thus he established the principal argument upon which moral theologians were to rely in the future when treating of venereal acts between members of the same sex. Although his classification of the various *peccata contra naturam* implies that different homosexual acts may vary in gravity, each act in itself is gravely sinful,[1] and discrimination between the species no longer serves the purpose of the confessional, as it did in the case of the Penitentials, or even for Leo IX.

With this account of the argument developed by the *Doctor Angelicus* we may draw to a close our survey of ecclesiastical legislation, teaching, and opinion, mentioning by way of conclusion the references made to homosexual practices by two of his contemporaries. Havelock Ellis states that 'at the end of [the thirteenth] century (about 1294) Alain de Lille was impelled to write a book, *De Planctu Naturæ*, in order to call attention to the prevalence of homosexual feeling; he also associated the neglect of women with sodomy'.[2] This, however, gives quite a wrong

---

[1] Cf. also the *Summa c. Gentiles*, iii. 122; also *Constit. Alex. episc. Coventr.* (1237), xx, *de luxuria* and *de pœnit.* (Migne, op. cit., xxiii, coll. 436, 438).

[2] Op. cit., ii, p. 36.

impression of Alain's treatise (written partly in prose and partly in poetry),[1] the theme of which is the complaint of Nature against all who deviate from the natural modes of conduct and intercourse, by the observance of which Man glorifies his Creator and attains true happiness and fulfilment in life. In other words, *De Planctu Naturæ* is an illustration, couched in somewhat euphuistic language, of the consequences of departing from the order of right reason which Aquinas had extolled. Inevitably the sodomists come in for the denunciations of Justice; we are told that 'Paris with Paris devises monstrous and unspeakable acts',[2] and that 'the human race, derogate from its high birth, commits monstrous acts in its union of genders, and perverts the rules of love by a practice of extreme and abnormal irregularity',[3] while maidens are neglected, and the kisses lie untouched upon their lips. But other vices—intemperance, gluttony, avarice, pride, and the rest—are castigated no less severely than sodomy, upon which Alain lays no special emphasis. His book is very far from being, as Ellis implies, a treatise on homosexual practices, nor is there any reliable evidence to show that these were specially prevalent at the time. From a literary standpoint *De Planctu Naturæ* is interesting, but as a serious contribution to the subject of our study its value is limited.

Finally we may note the four reasons given by Albert the Great, why the *peccata contra naturam*, and especially sodomy, are more to be detested than all other sins. First, they proceed from a burning frenzy (*ardor*) which subverts the order of nature; secondly, they are distinguished by their disgusting foulness—yet for all that, are found more often among persons of high degree than among those of low estate; thirdly, those who have once become addicted to these vices seldom succeed in shaking them off, so tenaciously do they cling; and lastly, they are as contagious as

---

[1] For the text, see Migne, *Patr. Lat.*, ccx; *De Planctu Naturæ* has been translated by Douglas M. Moffat, *The Complaint of Nature* (Yale Studies in English, xxxvi), New York, 1908.

[2] D. M. Moffat, op. cit., p. 4 (Migne, *P.L.*, col. 431).

[3] *Ibid.*, p. 36 (Migne, *P.L.*, col., 449).

any disease, and rapidly spread from one to another.[1] Like the intemperate polemic of Peter Damiani this catalogue, though penned by a greater and more liberal thinker, plainly depicts the kind of emotional reaction which homosexual acts could inspire in the mediæval ecclesiastical mind, conditioned as it had been to such an attitude by certain *a priori* assumptions which had been universally endorsed during the centuries which have now been briefly reviewed.

---

[1] *In evang. Luc.*, xvii. 29.

V

THE MEDIÆVAL SITUATION

WE have now examined the chief factors which contributed to the formation of the Western Christian attitude to homosexual practices, and have traced a cumulative process of development in which many diverse influences played their part—the post-exilic Jewish reinterpretation of the Sodom story, pagan and Christian Roman law, the legislation of Church councils and synods, the penitential system in one phase of its evolution, and the teaching of theologians and pastors. By the end of the thirteenth century the tradition was fully formed; it continued dominant in Europe for the next five hundred years at least, and is still powerful in the Anglo-Saxon countries, though it has from time to time been assailed as unworthy of an enlightened civilization.

Two points relative to the formation and effect of this tradition have been singled out for critical attention. First, it has been alleged that homosexual practices were more prevalent during the Middle Ages than is commonly supposed to have been the case. If this is true, it is of considerable significance for the social historian, and has a bearing also upon our interpretation and evaluation of theology and ecclesiastical legislation. Obviously the question is too large to admit of full investigation here, but an examination of the common opinion that the Normans were specially inclined to homosexual practices and introduced them into the lands which they conquered may prove useful in testing the particular force of this contention, and thus afford some guidance for a general assessment of the situation.

Secondly, it is not infrequently asserted that religious fanaticism and obscurantism have been mainly responsible for the antagonism towards the homosexual which has been a feature of the Western attitude, and which still largely determines public opinion and finds expression in law and in social sanctions. It is a commonplace of most arguments in defence of the homosexual and his right to engage in physical acts appropriate to his condition that the existing discriminations against him are survivals of barbarism and ecclesiastical bigotry. In support of this it is usually alleged that the mediæval Church constantly and relentlessly persecuted with a furious zeal those who indulged (or were believed to indulge) in homosexual acts, that it branded the heretic with an opprobrious epithet denoting a supposed addiction to sodomy, and by its general attitude made the cultivation of a more liberal and humane feeling impossible. It is important for our present study that these charges should be examined, as far as the evidence allows.

1. THE NORMANS

Havelock Ellis notes (without citing his authority for the statement) that homosexual practices flourished among the Normans, as among other warlike peoples,[1] and Mr. G. Rattray Taylor observes that a 'marked increase in homosexuality' [that is, in homosexual acts] 'which occurred in the twelfth century is commonly attributed to the Norman invasion'[2]—though he himself discounts this theory, and prefers to explain the alleged increase as a result of the repressive sexual morality inculcated by the Church. Contemporary records, on the other hand, contain nothing to suggest that sodomy was prevalent under William I or his predecessors, or that the conquerors of Gaul, England, and Sicily introduced it into the territories which they annexed. How, then, did the idea originate that the Normans had a peculiar propensity for homosexual indulgence, as a result of which a general increase in vicious practices took place in the twelfth century ?

If it could be traced to its source, there is little doubt that this idea would prove to be nothing more than a large and

---

[1] Op. cit., ii, p. 9.   [2] Op. cit., p. 34.

unwarranted inference from the lives and conduct of two sons of
the Conqueror, William Rufus and Robert, Duke of Normandy,
and the character of their courts. Concerning Robert the evidence
is uncertain; his marriage and numerous amours show that he was
definitely not an invert, but it has been suggested that he brought
back from the crusades a liking for homosexual practices. Ordericus Vitalis records that on his return he 'desperately (*damnabiliter*)
abandoned himself to indolence and effeminacy (*mollities*)',[1] and
that during his time vice was rampant in Normandy: 'The Venus
of Sodom stalked boldly in the midst of such scenes with her
wanton enticements, defiling the effeminate, who were fit only
to be burnt'.[2] This, however, can hardly refer to more than the
manners of Robert's immediate *entourage*.

There is no doubt, on the other hand, that William Rufus was
an invert. He was unmarried, and there is not the slightest hint of
his having mistresses or children;[3] moreover, his personal morals
are well attested: Freeman says that he 'stands well nigh alone in
bringing back the foulest vices of heathendom into a Christian
land'.[4] Yet even he was not 'refused burial in consecrated
ground', as Mr. Taylor alleges, because of his homosexual
practices, since there was no formal pretext for such a refusal; he
was interred within the Old Minster at Winchester, but without
religious rites—which was tantamount to a 'popular [that is,
unofficial] excommunication'. The Burial Service was withheld,
however, primarily on account of his blasphemy and contempt
of holy things and persons, and not because of his vicious life.[5]
As the man was, so was his court. Ordericus Vitalis states that
'the effeminate predominated everywhere and revelled without
restraint, while filthy catamites, fit only to perish in the flames,

---

[1] *Hist. Eccl.*, x. 16.

[2] Ibid., viii. 4.

[3] E. A. Freeman, *The Reign of William Rufus* (Oxford, 2 vols., 1882), ii, pp.
502–503.

[4] Op. cit., i, p. 157; cf. i, p. 147 ; also E. A. Freeman, *The History of the
Norman Conquest* (Oxford, 6 vols.), v, p. 72 and n. 1.

[5] See E. A. Freeman, *The Reign of William Rufus*, ii, p. 340.

abandoned themselves shamefully to the foulest practices of Sodom';[1] and William of Malmesbury tells the same tale.[2]

When Henry I, William Rufus's successor, came to the throne he addressed himself immediately and energetically to the task of cleaning up the court,[3] and two years after his accession, in 1102, a large mixed council assembled at Westminster for the reform of ecclesiastical and moral abuses. Among the canons enacted there were two which dealt specifically with homosexual offences. The first of these provided as follows:

> CONC. LONDIN. 28: 'In this council, those who commit the shameful sin of sodomy, and especially those who of their own free will take pleasure in doing so, were condemned by a weighty anathema, until by penitence and confession they should show themselves worthy of absolution. As for anyone who is found guilty of this crime, it was resolved that if he were an ecclesiastic he should not be promoted to any higher rank, and should be deposed from his present order; while if he were a layman he should be deprived of his legal status and dignity in the whole realm of England. And let none but the bishop presume to give absolution for this offence, save in the case of those who are members of the regular clergy.'[4]

The second[5] ordered the excommunication to be published every Sunday in all churches throughout the land, presumably in order that none should be ignorant of the censure passed by the leaders of Church and State upon the vices of the last reign, and should fail to take warning accordingly. This, however, was not immediately done, the reason given by Archbishop Anselm being that the canons needed more careful drafting and some revision before publication.[6] Meanwhile he advises an archdeacon named

---

[1] *Hist. Eccl.* viii. 10; cf. xi. 11, and William of Malmesbury, *Hist. Mod.* i.
[2] *Chron.* iv. 314; cf. 316; cf. also E. A. Freeman, *The Reign of William Rufus*, i, p. 159.
[3] Cf. William of Malmesbury, *Chron.* v. 393.
[4] Text in Mansi, op. cit., xx, col. 1152. The saving clause at the end was added to allow regulars to be absolved by their own superiors.
[5] *Conc. Londin.* 29 (Mansi, ibid.).
[6] *Epist.* iii. 62 (Migne, *Patr. Lat.*, clix, col. 94).

William how to deal with offenders—the regulation reserving all cases for the attention of the bishop being not yet in force:

EPIST. iii. 62; '. . . Concerning those who have committed the sin of Sodom either before or after the excommunication, not knowing that it had been promulgated, the sentence in both cases will be equal and similar if they confess and seek to do penance. You will assign penances at your discretion, taking into consideration the age of the offenders, the duration of the sin, and whether or not they have wives; and also how you see them performing their penance, and what promise they show of true amendment thereafter. It must be remembered that this sin has been publicly committed to such an extent that it scarcely makes anyone blush, and that many have fallen into it in ignorance of its gravity. As for those who defile themselves with this sin after learning of the excommunication, they ought to be dealt with more severely by way of penance. But we leave this to your discretion on the lines suggested.'[1]

The canon in question was not framed, as it has sometimes been stated,[2] only to deal with a 'failing of the priesthood', for it applied to clergy and laity alike. It is interesting to note, however, that as far as the former are concerned it seems to have been immediately successful, for a council held at Westminster in the year 1108 for the reform of clerical morals made no further enactments against sodomy, though it dealt fully with breaches of the rule of chastity.

This in itself indicates how little the example of William Rufus and his circle had really affected the rank and file of the English clergy and monastics. But the reactions inspired by the wreck of the *Blanche-Nef* in 1120, when William, Henry's heir, perished with a number of young nobles, suggest that suspicions of the court and the nobility still lingered, and may not perhaps have been altogether unjustified. It was alleged that most of those aboard the ill-fated craft were addicted to sodomy, but the testimony of the chroniclers is conflicting. Ordericus Vitalis states

---

[1] Text in Migne, *P.L.*, clix, coll. 95–96.
[2] E.g., by G. R. Taylor, op. cit., p. 34.

that certain persons left the ship before it sailed 'because they perceived therein an intemperate crowd of lascivious and showy young men',[1] and moralizes to the effect that the wicked commonly continue in their transgressions until they are brought to ruin. Gervase of Canterbury speaks of the prince's companions as 'puffed up with pride and defiled with every kind of lust and licence',[2] and William of Nangis asserts plainly that all who started on the voyage were sodomists.[3] In his *History*, Henry of Huntingdon makes a similar charge: of those who were drowned, 'all or most were said to have been tainted with the sin of sodomy. Behold the terrible vengeance of God!'[4]—but 'in another work, where he is avowedly speaking more especially from the moralist's point of view, he speaks of them in wholly different terms'.[5] Matthew Paris, on the other hand, is inclined to regard these accusations as nothing more than a French calumny,[6] and William of Malmesbury does not so much as allude to the opinion that the disaster was a Divine judgement upon a boat-load of sodomists.[7] Faced with these various assertions, denials, and imputations, it is clear that great caution should be exercised in venturing to pronounce upon the extent of homosexual practices in England twenty years after the death of William Rufus. It seems probable, however, on a general consideration of the evidence available, that his vices had neither a wide nor a lasting influence. Certainly there are no further references to sodomy at this time.

To conclude: the increase in homosexual practices in this country during the eleventh century alleged to have been due to Norman influence is found, upon investigation, to rest upon nothing more substantial than the personal conduct of William

---

[1] *Hist. Eccl.*, xii. 25.

[2] *Chron.*, in Rolls series, ed. W. Stubbs (London, 2 vols., 1879), ii, p. 92.

[3] *Chron.*, under A.D. 1120.

[4] *Hist.* vii.

[5] See Kate Norgate, in *Dict. Natnl. Biog.* (William, s. of Henry I), lxi, p. 337b. The work in question is the *Epist. ad Walter.*, in which Henry describes the character of the prince.

[6] *Hist. Angl.* i. 230.   [7] *Chron.* v. 419.

Rufus and the character of his court and companions in the thirteen years of his reign which brought that century to its close. He seems to have attracted and surrounded himself with compliant associates who readily fell in with his ways, with the result that in certain circles homosexual practices simply became fashionable for a time. This does not mean, as Mr Gordon Westwood says, that 'the Normans who settled in England after the conquest were known to have had a number of homosexuals among them',[1] for there is no proof that such was the case. It only shows how adaptable and accommodating the courtier and the libertine can be when convenience or self-interest require. But there is no reason to assume, against all the historical evidence, that the vices of the court or of a coterie of nobles and their sycophants were imitated in the country at large; perhaps there were those (as Anselm suggests[2]) who sinned after the royal example, thinking that what was now done openly in high places could hardly be counted very reprehensible—but they were doubtless but few. Nor should a disproportionate significance be attached to a temporary change in the conventions of sexual behaviour favoured by a dissolute minority; still less ought the practices of princes such as Robert of Normandy and William Rufus to be made the ground for attributing their depravity to the whole of their race.

2. Aristotelian Studies and Homosexual Practices in Paris

In the year 1210 a council held at Paris condemned certain works which purported to be written by Aristotle.[3] Two years later another council at Paris affirmed the third Lateran Council's decree[4] against sodomists,[5] and this was followed in 1214 by a similar step on the part of a council at Rouen.[6] Between these

---

[1] *Society and the Homosexual* (London, 1952), p. 101.
[2] See above, p. 125.
[3] *Conc. Paris.* (1210), ii (Mansi, op. cit., xxii, col. 804).
[4] *Conc. III Lateran.* (1179), 3rd sess., 11.
[5] *Conc. Paris.* (1212), ii. 21.
[6] *Conc. Rotomag.* (1214), ii. 24.

events there is no apparent connexion, but Dr Stanley-Jones has advanced the suggestion that, taken together, they throw considerable light upon the question of homosexual practices in mediæval times, and in support of this view has elaborated an ingenious thesis to prove that the action of the council of 1210 created a situation which made that of the councils of 1212 and 1214 imperative.[1]

It is well known that the Aristotelian philosophy, which was one of the most potent factors in the great intellectual advance of the thirteenth century, and provided the foundation and the framework upon which Albert the Great and Thomas Aquinas constructed the imposing edifice of the scholastic theology, entered Europe from the East by way of Arabian and Moorish channels. But the Aristotelianism with which the West became acquainted by these circuitous means was not the pure thought of the Philosopher. The Mohammedans first encountered his works and those of his Greek commentators in Syrian versions of an eclectic and undoubtedly Neo-Platonized character, and these were translated into Arabic under the encouragement of the rulers of Baghdad. Thus what passed into Arabian philosophy was not the unadulterated Aristotle, but the substance of his teaching coloured, interpreted, and modified by later Greek and Syrian thought; and it was to this orientalized version of the Stagirite that European scholars were introduced through the medium of the editions and commentaries of the Mohammedan philosophers, and in particular those of Ibn Rushd or Averroes, which were rendered into Latin.

The first works bearing Aristotle's name to reach Paris, however, were based on paraphrases (not translations) made by the eleventh-century Arabian scholar Ibn Sina, or Avicenna. These and other "Aristotelian" treatises and commentaries tended to emphasize those elements in the Philospher's teaching which were most markedly at variance with Christian doctrine, such as the eternity of matter, the unity of the active intellect, and the denial

---

[1] See D. Stanley-Jones, op. cit., pp. 14–17.

of personal immortality and of the creation of the universe by a personal act *ex nihilo*. The introduction of this orientalized presentation of Aristotelianism into the Parisian schools resulted in an outbreak of free thought and scepticism. One of those chiefly involved in this intellectual revolt was Amauri de Bene, whose errors and those of his followers were condemned by the council of 1210 already mentioned;[1] the same council also proscribed certain *libri naturales*, which were probably works attributed to Aristotle and derived from Arabic paraphrases of *De Anima*, the *Physics*, and perhaps part of the *Metaphysics*.

According to Dr Stanley-Jones, this local condemnation of Averroistic or Avicennistic versions of Aristotle left the field clear 'for the intensive study of Plato'; and he continues: 'The results of the new scholarship were alarming: instantly it was seen that the deeper passages in the Platonic dialogues could admit of only one interpretation, and impetus was given for the emergence of the hidden strains of homosexuality that lie endemic in all centres of population'.[2] This, in his view, explains the action taken by the ecclesiastical authorities: 'Within three years of the ban on Aristotle, the same[3] Council at Paris enacted the death penalty[4] for sexually inverted practices, which was reasserted at Rouen two years later'.[5] Finally, however, it is alleged that 'prompted by the desperate situation created by the rediscovery of Pagan morality, the University of Paris, in 1225,[6] allowed the study of Aristotle's works as the lesser of two evils, and it was thus that the system of Aristotle, which had maintained a position on terms approaching equality with that of Plato during the four hundred years that had elapsed since the time of Charlemagne,

---

[1] *Conc. Paris.* (1210)—see Mansi, op. cit., xxii, col. 809; cf. *Conc. IV Lateran.* (1215), ch. 2.

[2] Op. cit., p. 16.

[3] The council of 1212 was, of course, in fact quite distinct from that of 1210, and was convened for a different purpose.

[4] The canon in question, as we shall see, actually made no reference to the death penalty.

[5] Op. cit., p. 16.

[6] *Sic*; the actual date was 1255.

passed with undisputed supremacy into the thirteenth and four-
teenth centuries. . . .'¹ Such, in outline, is Dr Stanley-Jones's
theory, as he propounds it. He holds that 'it was the sympathetic
attitude of Plato, or rather his active enthusiasm for sexual
heterodoxy'² which was directly responsible for the fact that
despite its first suspicions the mediæval Church eventually
accepted Aristotelianism—for 'the philosophy of Plato . . . could
not without grievous mutilation have been separated from the
tolerant approval of masculine romance which was native to his
race, and in no circumstances could the Academic tradition have
been incorporated into the Christian faith without explosive
reaction with the homosexual taboo of the Mosaic Law'.³ Does
the evidence support this argument?

To examine all the questions raised by this theory would carry
us far outside the range of our subject, for the purpose of which it
is only necessary to comment briefly upon certain points. First, it
hardly conveys an accurate impression of the state of early scholastic studies to say that during the ninth and following centuries
the Platonic and Aristotelian systems flourished together 'on
terms approaching equality'. True, there was no rivalry between
them, but this does not mean that either exerted an influence in
any way comparable to that which it possessed later. Until the
second half of the twelfth century the acquaintance of the school-
men with both philosophers was very limited, and was derived
mainly at second hand from translations, commentary, and
similar sources. Most of what was known about Plato, for
instance, came from reproductions of Platonic (and more often,
Neo-Platonic) teaching in Latin authors such as Cicero, Apuleius
(*De Dogmate Platonis*), Augustine, Macrobius, and Boethius;
from renderings of the Neo-Platonists, and of Arabic works
inspired by their influence; and from versions of the Pseudo-
Dionysius. The *Timæus,* at least in part, was available in the
Latin translation of Chalcidius and enjoyed, with the *Phædo* and
the *Meno,* a small circulation; but the *Symposium,* the *locus*

¹ Op. cit., pp. 16–17.   ² Ibid., p. 15.   ³ Ibid., p. 16.

classicus of the Platonic conception of love, was virtually unknown. Thus the suggestion that the ban on Aristotle in 1210 left the field clear for 'an intensive study of Plato' fails to take into account the real position of Platonic studies at the time.

Moreover, had the scholars of Paris turned their attention from the Peripatetic to the Academic philosophy, it is very doubtful whether they could have discovered in the meagre corpus of Platonic material which lay to hand anything likely to encourage a revival of the idealized *paiderastia* extolled in one or two of the dialogues. Certainly they would have found there no incitement to indulge in the homosexual practices which are alleged to have called forth the censure of the Church authorities—and it may be observed that they, no less than the philosopher of later times, would have been amazed and perplexed to learn that Plato's 'active enthusiasm for sexual heterodoxy' was so intrinsic a part of his system that its displacement would amount to a 'grievous mutilation'. Indeed, there is little or nothing that he said about homosexual love which cannot, *mutatis mutandis*, be applied with equal or greater force to the relation between man and woman; the "homosexual" allusions in certain of his works are in the strict sense of the word accidental, and are due simply to the social (and sexual) conventions and theories of his time—they have no universal validity.

Five years after the decree of 1210 the statutes of the University of Paris banned the *Physics* and the *Metaphysics* of Aristotle, and in 1231 these interdicts were provisionally renewed by a decretal of Gregory IX setting up a commission to scrutinize the editions concerned, and ordering that they must not be used 'until they shall have been examined and purged of all heresy'.[1] This commission accomplished nothing, but the original prohibitions, though never rescinded (Urban IV, in 1263, still speaks as if they were effective), were ignored in practice, and in 1255 Aristotle's works were prescribed as text books in the faculty of Arts at Paris.[2] Thus there is no question of the authorities permitting a

---

[1] See H. Rashdall (ed. F. M. Powicke and A. B. Emden), *The Universities of Europe in the Middle Ages* (Oxford, 3 vols., 1936), i, p. 357.

[2] Ibid., i. p. 358.

resumption of Aristotelian studies as a counter-measure to the alleged effect of Platonism in encouraging homosexual practices. The truth is that Aristotle proved too strong for those who opposed him, and could no longer be ignored; furthermore, the work of Albert the Great and Thomas Aquinas, aided by the provision of accurate texts free from Arabic glosses, made it unnecessary to regard his writings with the suspicion which at first had been fully warranted.

Having shown that the study of Plato did not temporarily succeed the study of Aristotle at the University of Paris, we have still to consider the second strand in Dr Stanley-Jones's argument —namely, that a notable increase in homosexual practices coincided with the imposition of the ban upon the Averroistic versions of the works of the Stagirite. This view had already been advanced by Havelock Ellis, who stated that 'in France in the thirteenth century the Church was so impressed by the prevalence of homosexuality that it reasserted the death penalty for sodomy at the Councils of Paris (1212) and Rouen (1214)'.[1] A review of the evidence, however, shows that there is no foundation for this statement.

The council of Paris in 1212 was convened principally to deal with the discipline of the clergy, and of monastics of both sexes. Like other mediæval councils which addressed themselves to this task, its legislation was voluminous, and in all eighty-nine canons were enacted. Of these, however, two alone relate to homosexual matters, and one of these concerns women; nuns are required to sleep *singulæ . . . in lectis suis, non binæ,* according to the Benedictine rule—and a gloss repeats the order from the same source that lamps must be left burning in dormitories during the night.[2] The other canon applies to the clergy; regulars are likewise forbidden to lie two in one bed, and then comes the enactment to which Ellis and Dr Stanley-Jones refer:

CONC. PARIS. (1212), ii. 21: 'As for members of the secular clergy who commit incontinency against nature, on account of which the

1 Op. cit., ii, p. 37.
2 *Conc. Paris.* (1212), iii. 2 (Mansi, op. cit., xxii, col. 849).

wrath of God came upon the children of disobedience, and he consumed five cities with fire: let it be decreed (in accordance with the Lateran Council)[1] that if they are caught they are to be degraded from the clergy or consigned to a monastery to do penance; and we consider that this law in all its rigour ought to be applied much more to the regular clergy, who have entered upon the way of perfection.'[2]

When the canons passed at this council are compared with the one hundred and fourteen made at the Council of Rouen two years later, it will be seen that the latter assembly did little more than re-enact *en bloc,* with certain amendments, the laws put forth by the Council of Paris; the twenty-five additional canons for which it was responsible are explained by the filling of some gaps left by the Paris legislation, by the division of some canons into two, and by the appending of a supplementary section of fourteen canons at the end.[3] One of the canons divided was that relating to homosexual offences by clerics, the prohibition of sleeping together[4] being separated from the enforcement of the third Lateran Council's decree against *incontinentia contra naturam;*[5] in both cases, however, the wording itself was left virtually unchanged, while the canon dealing with nuns was repeated without alteration.[6]

It is somewhat misleading, therefore, to treat these two councils as though they had acted independently; what really happened was that the measures taken at Paris to secure discipline in that diocese were afterwards made effective within the diocese of Rouen. In both cases the action was strictly local; neither council had national, much less ecumenical status, and to represent their comparatively domestic concerns as the affair of the Church at large is to invest them with an exaggerated importance. This in itself diminishes somewhat the force of the argument which we have under examination.

---

[1] *Conc. III Lateran.* (1179), 3rd sess., 11.
[2] Text in Mansi, op. cit., xxii, col. 831.
[3] See Mansi, op. cit., xxii, coll. 897–898.
[4] *Conc. Rotomag.* (1214), ii. 23 (Mansi, op. cit., xxii, col. 910).
[5] Ibid., ii. 24 (Mansi, ibid.).
[6] Ibid., ii. 32 (Mansi, op. cit., xxii, col. 932).

If the significance of these councils has been over-rated, what of their attitude to homosexual practices? When we consider their legislation in its entirety (bearing in mind that the Council of Rouen did little more than repeat what the Council of Paris had done) we find nothing which even remotely suggests that the Church was in any way 'impressed by the prevalence of homosexuality', or that an 'alarming' increase had occurred in the incidence of sodomy at this time. It was almost inevitable that councils concerned with the regulation of clerical discipline should refer to homosexual practices, for these were sins of the flesh to which the celibate and those who were segregated in one-sex institutions were specially liable. But the routine enforcement of a decree made nearly forty years before against such practices hardly conveys the impression that there was any agitation about the matter in ecclesiastical circles. To see the question in its true perspective, it is only necessary to contrast the action of the Council of Paris in re-enacting the provisions of the third Lateran Council as one item of legislation among eighty-nine (in the case of the Council of Rouen, one among one hundred and fourteen) with the action of the Council of Naplouse[1] in passing a series of canons to deal with a serious outbreak of immorality.

Two further points may be noted in conclusion. First, the Councils of Paris and Rouen did not reassert the death penalty for sodomy—a penalty which had never, in fact, been imposed by ecclesiastical authority, and which the Church had no power to carry out; they only punished offenders with degradation and penance. Secondly (to return to the alleged connexion between the canons against homosexual practices and the suppression of Aristotelian studies), it is interesting to note that the followers of Amauri, the sceptics who were influenced by the orientalized versions of Aristotle, were themselves accused of immoral principles. Cæsarius of Heisterbach alleges that they had said: 'If any one is in the Holy Spirit . . . and commits fornication or is polluted with any other kind of pollution, it is not sin to him'[2]—

---

[1] See above, pp. 95 f.
[2] *Mirac. et Hist. Mem.* v. 32; cf. Mansi, op. cit., xxii, col. 803.

a proposition which would serve to justify homosexual practices on grounds not remotely connected with Platonism. It is doubtful, however, whether such an assertion was ever made by the free-thinkers of Paris, and Cæsarius was probably repeating malicious gossip about them.[1]

Having shown that the temporary proscription of Aristotelian studies at Paris did not result in the encouragement of Platonism, and that there is no foundation for the opinion that homosexual practices were unusually prevalent in France at the beginning of the thirteenth century, it is clear that despite its ingenuity Dr Stanley-Jones's theory must be rejected.[2]

3. HERITE AND BOUGRE

Dr Kinsey states that 'in mediæval European history there are abundant records of death imposed upon males for sexual activities with other males',[3] but in support of this assertion he adduces nothing that can be regarded as conclusive evidence. He merely cites passages from Havelock Ellis, alleging that Louis IX of France consigned sodomists to the flames,[4] and from Wester-marck, declaring that in the Middle Ages homosexual practices were so closely connected with heterodoxy in belief that 'heretics were as a matter of course accused of unnatural vice'.[5] Neither writer, however, gives any satisfactory documentation for his statement, and nothing short of a thorough investigation of mediæval trials for heresy could show to what extent Wester-marck's generalization is warranted. It is certain that no imputation of sexual immorality was made against many of those who

---

[1] See H. Rashdall, op. cit., i, p. 355, n. 1.

[2] Having criticized adversely Dr Stanley-Jones's theory, I would wish to pay tribute to his unremitting efforts to promote consideration of the problem of homosexuality, and to secure justice and understanding for the invert.

[3] Op. cit., p. 484.   [4] Op. cit., ii, p. 347.

[5] *The Origin and Development of the Moral Ideas*, ii, pp. 486 ff.; cf. *Christianity and Morals*, pp. 370–371; *Early Beliefs and their Social Influence*, p. 129; also H. C. Lea, *A History of the Inquisition of the Middle Ages* (London, 3 vols., 1888), i, p. 115, n.

were charged with error in matters of faith; and it is equally certain that some heretics were guilty of advancing theories, if not indulging in practices, which contravened the moral law. But there is no proof that large numbers of persons were put to death simply and solely because they had committed some homosexual offence. Indeed, it is doubtful whether such delinquents were ever handed over by the Church to the civil power after conviction in the ecclesiastical courts—and it is to be noted that the various canons against sodomists go no further than the imposition of an appropriate penance. Generally, it seems that in practice homosexual offenders only became liable to the severity of the law if their behaviour was attributable to heretical ideas, or if immorality in conduct was accompanied by grave error in belief. While it is impossible, therefore, to accept what Dr Kinsey says as an accurate statement of fact, his assertion draws attention to two questions which bear directly upon the subject of this study and require examination—namely, the attitude of the developing French law towards sodomists, and the extent to which *bougre* and *herite* were actually identified in mediæval thought.

One of the most dangerous and persistent perils with which the early and the mediæval Church had to contend was that of Manicheism—the "aboriginal heresy", as it has been called—an eclectic religious and philosophical system which arose in Persia during the latter part of the third century. For our purpose the briefest outline of its progress will suffice. After the "martyrdom" of its founder, Mani, at the hands of the Magi whose doctrines he had challenged, his adherents dispersed, making their way westwards into the Roman empire. Some introduced the Manichean teachings into north Africa, where they achieved a notable success at first; finally, however, they had to admit defeat by the Church, whereupon they crossed to Italy and resumed their missionary labours there. As a result of prolonged joint exertions by the spiritual and civil powers they were eventually suppressed, but not extinguished, during the pontificate of Gregory I.

For some four centuries Manicheism lay dormant in Italy, while in the East it became aggressive. Others of the Manichean dispersion had propagated their tenets in Cappadocia and Armenia, and notably in Bulgaria, where the exiles had settled in large numbers. There a reformed Manicheism was evolved, in which the leadership of Mani and some of his more obscure and complicated doctrines were rejected—just as a gradual westernization of the Manichean system was taking place at the same time among the Italian members of the sect who had gone underground after their suppression in the early years of the seventh century. The result of this development was the emergence in Bulgaria of the Paulician heresy—while the vigour of the movement as a whole is attested by the appearance of dissenters within it, leading to the separation of the Bogomils at the close of the tenth century.

From Bulgaria the Paulician doctrines began gradually to spread westwards. This infiltration led to a revival of the Manicheism which had for so long lain dormant in Italy, and from there the heresy began to extend into Provence and the south of France. At the same time Germany and northern France, and to a very limited degree England, became infected with the new teachings, and from about the year 1000 there were repeated outbreaks of heretical activity. In the north, however, the "Bulgarians" gained but a slight hold and were easily suppressed, whereas in the south the movement assumed formidable proportions, and culminated in the Albigensian heresy, the destruction of which forms a notable and not altogether creditable passage in the annals of the mediæval Church.

Since the "Bulgarian" (that is, the Paulician or Manichean) heresy was in many respects the heresy *par excellence* of the Middle Ages, it is hardly surprising that all heretics indiscriminately (and often not without good reason) were termed "Bulgarians" (*Bulgari*, *Boulgres*—which were corrupted into *Bugari* and *Bougres*), and that *bougre* thus came to be synonymous with *herite*. How then did *bougre* acquire the meaning of its modern English equivalent, and become associated with sodomy rather than with heresy? One explanation which has been advanced is that in order to denigrate the heretics the Church imputed to them practices of which they were wholly innocent; thus the

Albigenses have been represented as innocuous puritans and religious reformers whose reputation for sexual asceticism 'was turned by malicious and intentional fabrication, and without a shred of supporting evidence, into a stigma of unnatural vice'.[1] This charge implies that the Albigenses were actually not heretics, and that the calumny of homosexual vice had to be invented in order to provide a pretext for their extermination as 'a political menace to the Church'.

The transparency of this allegation is sufficiently demonstrated by some of the tenets of these particular heretics, as stated at the third Lateran Council:[2] they maintained the dualistic principle of Manicheism, which involved the proposition that matter is evil; they rejected the Eucharist; they disowned the Old Testament, its God, and its Law; and they denied the efficacy of infant baptism, and the resurrection of the body. Nor were these their only errors. They professed a docetic Christology,[3] and some even taught that the Christ of the Gospels was an emanation of the Spirit of Evil. They repudiated the Church's sacramental means of grace and the doctrine of salvation by faith, and substituted for them the ceremony of the *Consolamentum*—holding, contrary to Catholic principle, that the efficacy of this rite depended upon the purity of the officiating Perfectus. They depreciated public worship and all ecclesiastical ordinances; and they undoubtedly encouraged voluntary suicide by means of the discipline of self-starvation known as the *endura*. Confronted with so manifestly heretical a system, the main features of which were admitted without hesitation, it was quite unnecessary for the authorities to brand the Albigenses as sexually immoral in order to justify their suppression. Since fabrication of the charge of homosexual practices would, therefore, have been utterly pointless, we must ask whether it had not a foundation in fact.

When enumerating the heretical tenets of the Albigenses no

---

[1] D. Stanley-Jones, op. cit., p. 26.

[2] *Conc. Lateran.* (1179), 27.

[3] The Docetists, a very early sect of heretics, denied the reality of the Incarnation, and held that Christ's human body was merely a physical body in appearance.

mention was made of their attitude to sexual matters. They professed, it is true, to be advocates of chastity—but it was not
chastity as understood and taught by the Church. They were
opposed, not to coitus as such, but to procreation, since they
regarded the propagation of the species as wrong. So long as
sexual acts did not lead to conception, however, they did not
prohibit those below the highest rank of Initiate or Perfectus from
indulging in them. Fornication, in their view, was only an
isolated sin, but marriage was nothing less than a state of sin; hence
casual promiscuity, though never positively enjoined by the
Catharist authorities, was evidently not discouraged in the case of
those who belonged to the lesser grades of the sect, while homosexual acts themselves would not be denied the advantage of
freeing sexual pleasure from all risk of bringing children into the
world.

Holding such convictions about marriage and coitus, it is unlikely that the conduct of the heretics remained blameless in all
respects, and that the oft-repeated allegations of sodomy were unfounded. On the other hand, it must not be forgotten that homosexual practices were apparently never advocated, even though
they may have been condoned, and that by no means all the
Albigenses were guilty of the gross excesses with which they
were charged. Nevertheless, after a very judicious survey of the
evidence, Mr J. C. S. Runciman concludes that in the case of
adherents and Believers the accusations of debauchery and
sodomy were not, on the whole, unjustified, but that the Initiates
or Perfecti (as indeed their opponents admitted) were innocent of
the immoralities committed by the rest—though it seems that
they can hardly be acquitted of excusing in others what they did
not practise themselves. There was definitely among the Cathari
'an easygoing attitude about sexual morals, an attitude peculiarly
agreeable to the people of southern France'.[1]

While there is no doubt that the immorality of the Albigenses
was deliberately exaggerated for polemical and propaganda

[1] J. C. S. Runciman, *The Medieval Manichee* (Cambridge, 1947), p. 177; and see
pp. 176–179.

purposes, it is equally certain that the charge of homosexual practices was not entirely without foundation. But they were not attacked as heretics solely or even principally because of such practices; their offence was that their teaching on many cardinal points of doctrine was directly contrary to that of the Church, and it was for this reason that action was originally taken against them—only later did political questions arise. So too in the case of the Templars: there is little doubt that the accusations of unnatural vice levelled against the Order were justified—but it was not only because of this that measures were taken to suppress it, and that its members were brought to trial. Yet again, we hear of a peasant named Clementius of Bucy, near Soissons, who in 1125 gathered around him a band of followers whom Guibert of Nogent taxes with homosexual practices; but it is significant that they, too, held marriage and procreation to be crimes, regarded Christ's humanity as an illusion, and taught that the altar was 'the mouth of Hell'.[1]

There is no need to labour at greater length the fact that the charges of sodomy laid against the Albigenses and other heretics were no malicious fabrications invented to denigrate them and to justify their suppression. Contrary to what is commonly asserted by its critics, no heretic was ever automatically branded by the mediæval Church as a sodomist, nor were those who indulged in homosexual practices treated as heretics unless they were guilty also of grave error in matters of faith. In so far, therefore, as heresy and sodomy came to be identified in mediæval thought, the explanation is simply that during the Middle Ages many heretics (and among them the most notable and dangerous) were dualists, and propagated teaching about marriage and coitus which was repugnant not only to Christian doctrine but also to reason and human sentiment. Their theories found expression, not only in wild and defiant assertions calculated to subvert morality, but occasionally also in promiscuous orgies, while some construed them as justifications for homosexual practices; the Church's accusations, therefore, hardly amounted to more

---

[1] J. C. S. Runciman, op. cit., p. 120.

than a restatement of the tenets of the heretics, whose behaviour was assumed, reasonably enough, to conform to their creed. It was principally for their sexual antinomianism that the "Bulgarians" became notorious in the popular mind—though it was only a subsidiary and not a basic element in their teaching; and this explains how *bougre*, which at first simply denoted *herite*, gradually came to signify that class of heretic whose system tended to encourage or condone sodomy, and finally, any sodomite (as in modern usage), regardless of his religious views. There is evidence, too, that *bougre* had at first a much wider pejorative application; Matthew Paris, for instance, states that it was a common term for usurer—*usurarii, quos Franci Bugeros vulgariter appellant*;[1] but it has only survived in its narrower meaning.

In conclusion, let us glance at the attitude of the early French law towards homosexual offences. Havelock Ellis makes the curious statement that 'St Louis had handed over these sacrilegious offenders' [that is, sodomists] 'to the Church to be burned',[2] but there appears to be no evidence for this assertion; it may perhaps be due to an erroneous assumption that the code of law entitled *Les Établissements de Saint Louis* was actually promulgated by Louis IX. In fact, the *Établissements* (c. 1272) was the work of a jurist in the royal service who collected together the customary laws of Orleans, Anjou, and Maine, and added a few ordinances made by Louis himself; it was not compiled or issued by the king's authority, and most of its contents considerably antedate the thirteenth century. One of the items in this code, derived from the *Coutume de Touraine-Anjou*,[3] was directed against "Bulgarian" heretics, but its wording is ambiguous and might suggest that a distinction was intended between *bougre* and *herite*, whereas this is not really so:

ÉTAB. i. 90: 'If anyone is suspected of *bougrerie* the magistrate must seize him and send him to the bishop: and if he is convicted, he must

---

[1] See P. Viollet, *Les Établissements de St Louis* (Paris, 4 vols., 1881–1886), iv, p. 36.

[2] Op. cit., ii, p. 347.

[3] *C. de T.-A.*, 78; see Viollet, op. cit., iii, p. 50.

be burnt, and all his goods confiscated to the baron. And the heretic (*l'ome herite*) ought to be dealt with in the same way, when his offence has been proved, and all his goods confiscated to the baron.'[1]

There is no doubt that *bougrerie* here denotes the dualistic heresy of the Albigenses, while *l'ome herite* is simply a person guilty of other kinds of error. The fact that *bougre* had no definite homosexual significance at this time is evident from the collection entitled *Li Livres de Jostice et de Plet* which was probably compiled about the year 1260 by the legal school of Orleans. Several passages in this code refer to *bogrerie* in the sense of heresy,[2] but the one law dealing specifically with homosexual practices used the term *sodomite*:

> JOSTICE ET PLET, XVIII. xxiv. 22: 'Those who have been proved to be sodomites (*qui sont sodomite prouvé*) must lose their c——[?]. And if anyone commits this offence a second time, he must undergo mutilation (*il doit perdre membre*). And if he does it a third time, he must be burnt.'

An unusual feature of this statute is that it also deals with women:

> 'The woman who does this shall undergo mutilation (*perdre membre*) for the [first and second] offences (*à chescune foiz*), and on her third [conviction] must be burnt. And all the goods of such offenders shall be the king's.'[3]

Here we see the direct influence of the legislation of the Theodosian code upon the ancient customary law of Anjou, to which it had been transmitted through the Visigothic and the Carolingian laws. The death penalty is certainly prescribed, but only for a third offence; this provision, however, as we have already seen, had existed from the fourth century, and there is no evidence that

---

[1] Text in Viollet, op. cit., ii, pp. 147–148.
[2] Cf. I. iii. 7 and X. xix. 6–7; texts in P. N. Rapetti, *Li Livres de Jostice et de Plet* (Paris, 1850), pp. 12–13 and 215–216. Viollet (op. cit., i, p. 254) notes that in the *Jostice et Plet, bougre* means heretic, and that in the *Établissements* it has the same sense—'Il est hardi', he says, 'de traduire, dans les *Établissements, herite* par *sodomite*' (ibid., n. 1).
[3] Text in Rapetti, op. cit., pp. 279–280.

Louis IX was particularly assiduous in applying it. For instance, out of over fifteen hundred judgements pronounced in the Parlement, which then corresponded to the courts of the Queen's Bench and the Common Pleas, during his reign, only one makes any reference to sodomists—and this simply touches a matter of disputed criminal jurisdiction:

> LES OLIM, I, fol. 24 r⁰ (Parlement of Pentecost, 1261): 'Judgement pronounced on the claim of the bishop of Amiens against the town of Amiens, asserting that he had the right to judge sodomists (*sodomitici*); and on the counter claim by the burgesses of Amiens that the right of judgement belonged to them, and not to the bishop: A better case has been made for the town of Amiens than for the bishop; let the right of judgement upon the bodies of sodomists (*corpora sodomiticorum*) remain with the town.'[1]

In any case, the assertion that Louis 'handed over ... offenders to the Church to be burned' displays a strange ignorance of mediæval criminal law procedure, for the Church had no power to inflict capital punishment. Both the *Coutume de Touraine-Anjou* and the *Établissements* provide for heretics to be handed over for trial to the bishop, but the laws make it clear that convicted *bougres* must be handed back by the ecclesiastical authorities to the secular magistracy (*la joutise laie*) for execution.[2] In the case of sodomists the procedure is not laid down, and the dispute at Amiens throws no light upon the question—we do not know whether the citizens had established a right to exercise the jurisdiction normally belonging to the bishop, or whether he was attempting to encroach upon their powers. But whether sodomists were tried in the secular or the ecclesiastical courts, there is no doubt that the civil power had to carry out such punitive or capital sentences as the *Livres de Jostice et de Plet* impose. The Church could do no more than stipulate the performance of an

---

[1] Text in A. A. Beugnot, *Les Olim, ou Registres des Arrêts* (Paris, 1849), p. 136 (no. v); see also M. E. Boutaric, *Actes du Parlement de Paris* (Paris, 1863), p. 53 (no. 579).

[2] See *La Coutume de Touraine-Anjou*, 116 = *Les Établissements*, i. 127 (Viollet, op. cit, iii, p. 79 and ii, p. 240).

appropriate penance—and it is significant that none of the canons relating to sodomy do more than assign spiritual penalties; they do not direct that the offender must be brought to trial, or punished as the law requires. Ellis's statements, therefore, concerning Louis IX's methods with sodomists are incorrect in this particular matter, and it seems impossible to discover the grounds upon which he levels against this sovereign the general charge of being a *malleus sodomiticorum*.

VI

THE LAW IN ENGLAND

ONE of the earliest accounts of the English law is to be found in the treatise entitled *Fleta*,[1] which was probably composed about the year 1290 by a jurist at the court of Edward I. The penalty prescribed therein for homosexual offences is unique in the annals of jurisprudence:

> FLETA, xxxvii. 3: 'Those who have dealings with Jews or Jewesses, those who commit bestiality, and sodomists, are to be buried alive, after legal proof that they were taken in the act, and public conviction.'[2]

It is extremely improbable that this manner of death was ever inflicted upon sodomists in mediæval times. Burial alive for this crime was probably a penalty of Teutonic origin which had become embedded in some obscure legal tradition known to the author of *Fleta*, for Tacitus records that among the Germans of his day 'cowards and poor fighters and notorious evil-livers (*corpore infames*) are plunged in the mud of marshes with a hurdle on their heads'.[3]

Not long after the composition of *Fleta* another work appeared, inspired by the project of codifying the English law which is supposed to have emanated from Edward I himself. This was the compilation known as *Britton*, which was prepared and published with express authority, and probably came from the hand of Sir

---

[1] It is reputed to have been written during the imprisonment of the unknown author in the Fleet.

[2] *Fleta, seu Commentarius Juris Anglicani* (London, 1735), p. 84.

[3] *Germ.* 12.

John le Breton. In it the customary penalty for sodomy is laid down:

> BRITTON, i. 10: 'Let enquiry also be made of those who feloniously in time of peace have burnt others' corn or houses, and those who are attainted thereof shall be burnt, so that they may be punished in like manner as they have offended. The same sentence shall be passed upon sorcerers, sorceresses, renegades, sodomists, and heretics publicly convicted.'[1]

An ancient commentator[2] observes in this connexion that 'the enquirers of Holy Church shall make their inquests of sorcerers, sodomists, renegates, and misbelievers; and if they find any such, they shall deliver him to the king's court to be put to death. Nevertheless, if the king by inquest find any person guilty of such horrible sin, he may put them to death, as a good marshal of Christendom'.[3] This clarifies at any rate the procedure followed in England: the ecclesiastical courts were normally responsible for the trial of sodomists, and the function of the secular tribunal was to impose the penalty of the law upon those who were convicted by the spiritual authority. But although, generally speaking, the king's court was ancillary to the ecclesiastical courts in this matter, it had the power to act independently; consequently sodomy did not necessarily come within the cognizance of the Church.

The treatment of sodomists required by *Fleta* may safely be dismissed as a piece of legal archaism; and since Glanville makes no reference to homosexual practices in his treatise *De Legibus et Consuetudinibus Regni Angliæ,* we may assume that *Britton* represents the standard attitude to the subject on the part of mediæval English jurists. We have now to ask: Was the extreme penalty imposed by *Britton* ever enforced? Here the conclusion of two such authorities as Pollock and Maitland is valuable. They observe that in the Middle Ages sodomy appears to have been

---

[1] Text and translation in *Britton,* ed. F. M. Nichols (Oxford, 2 vols., 1865), i, pp. 41–42.
[2] MS "N" in F. M. Nichols' edition.
[3] See F. M. Nichols, op. cit., i, p. 42.

regarded in much the same way as sorcery. Concerning the latter, the thirteenth century 'seems to have been content to hold as an academic opinion that sorcerers, being heretics, ought to be burnt, if convicted by the courts of Holy Church; but no serious effort was made to put this theory into practice'. So too with sodomists—though as such they were not classed as heretics: they came under the jurisdiction of the ecclesiastical courts, and the prevailing view was that 'if the Church relinquished the offenders to the secular arm, they ought to be burnt'. But this was also largely an academic opinion, for the learned authors consider that as a matter of fact persons in England who were guilty of homosexual acts were not thus relinquished; and as 'an almost sufficient proof that the temporal courts had not punished [sodomy], and that no one had been put to death for it for a very long time past', they cite the preamble to the important statute of 1533 by which it was made a felony.[1]

This act ran as follows:

25 HENR. VIII. c. 6: 'Forasmuch as there is not yet sufficient and condign punishment appointed and limited by the due course of the Laws of this Realm, for the detestable and abominable Vice of Buggery committed with mankind or beast: It may therefore please the King's Highness, with the assent of his Lords spiritual and temporal, and the Commons of this present Parliament assembled, that it may be enacted by authority of the same, That the same offence be from henceforth adjuged Felony, and such order and form of process therein to be used against the offenders, as in cases of Felony at the Common-law. And that the offenders being hereof convict by Verdict, Confession, or Outlawry, shall suffer such pains of death, and losses, and penalties of their goods, chattels, debts, lands, tenements and hereditaments, as Felons be accustomed to doe according to the order of the Common-laws of this Realm. And that no person offending in any such offence, shall be admitted to his Clergy,[2] And that Justices of Peace shall have power and authority,

---

[1] See F. Pollock and F. W. Maitland, *The History of the English Law before the time of Edward I* (Cambridge, 2 vols., 1898), ii, pp. 556–557.

[2] That is, to Benefit of Clergy, by which persons in holy orders were exempted from the usual penalties imposed by the criminal law.

within the limits of their Commissions and Jurisdictions, to hear and determin the said offence, as they do use to doe in cases of other Felonies. This Act to endure till the last day of the next Parliament.'[1]

It is impossible to ascertain the precise reason for this enactment, which eschews the traditional appeal of legislators to the destruction of Sodom and Gomorrah, but it is probably not unconnected with Henry's policy of ecclesiastical readjustment necessitated by the new conception of the royal supremacy. Cases of sodomy were now removed entirely from the jurisdiction of the Church courts and were committed to the civil magistrates for trial, thus establishing as the rule a procedure which was perhaps exceptional in mediæval times—though it was always, as we have seen, within the competence of the king's court to take proceedings against sodomists independently of the spiritual authorities. Furthermore, such offenders were now included, with murderers and robbers below the rank of subdeacon,[2] in the category of those who might not claim Benefit of Clergy. Finally, the death penalty was imposed, though the manner of execution was not specified; in most cases it was presumably carried out by hanging.

It will be observed that during the previous two centuries *bougrerie* had lost its original connotation of "heresy", and that its English equivalent, "buggery", now included bestiality as well as sodomy. It seems that after the dualistic heresy had at last been suppressed, its popular designation was transferred to the homosexual acts which its perverse teaching on chastity was supposed to permit, if not to advocate, and was finally extended to include acts committed with animals. Thus a word which had at first indicated the provenance of heterodox beliefs came to signify in the technical usage of lawyers a crime, 'the very mention of which is a disgrace to human nature,'[3] and being banished from

---

[1] Text in E. Gibson, *Codex Juris Ecclesiastici Anglicani*, Tit. xlvii, c. 3 (Oxford, 2 vols., 1761, ii, p. 1080).

[2] Forbidden Benefit of Clergy by 4 Henr. VIII. c. 2, renewed by 23 Henr. VIII. c. 1.

[3] W. Blackstone, ed. J. Chitty, *Commentaries on the Laws of England* (London, 4 vols., 1826), iv, p. 215.

polite conversation, has been kept in currency by the abuse or the pleasantries of the vulgar.

The statute of 1533 was 'to endure till the last day of the next Parliament', and three further Acts renewed it for similar periods, each declaring that it was 'beneficial and profitable for the commonweale of this Realme'—or words to that effect;[1] then in 1541 it was again re-enacted, this time to 'continue and endure in force and strength, and be observed and kept for ever'.[2] In 1547 the first Parliament of Edward VI passed a comprehensive statute of repeal by which, *inter alia,* all the new felonies created in the last reign were abolished, including that of buggery established by the Act of 1533.[3] In 1548, however, the provisions of this Act were again given force by a new statute,[4] the following minor amendments being introduced: the penalty on conviction was to be death, but without loss of goods or land; the rights of the offender's wife and children, and of all lawful claimants upon his estate, were safeguarded; indictments had to be made within six months of the commission of the act in question; and no person due to benefit in the event of the death of the accused might be admitted to give evidence against him.

Mary's accession was marked by another comprehensive statute of repeal by which, among many other Acts, that of 1548 was rescinded;[5] and no steps were taken during her reign to introduce further legislation against those who were guilty of sodomy or bestiality—presumably because it was intended that with the restoration of the old religion such offences should again fall under the jurisdiction of the Church courts. In 1563, however, Elizabeth's second Parliament passed an Act[6] declaring that 'Sithence which Repeal so had and made, divers evil disposed persons have been the more bold to commit the said most horrible

---

[1] In 1536, by 28 Henr. VIII. c. 1, and again by 28 Henr. VIII. c. 6 (the former renewing the provision regarding Benefit of Clergy; the latter continuing the whole Act); and in 1539, by 31 Henr. VIII. c. 7.
[2] 32 Henr. VIII. c. 3.
[3] 1 Edw. VI. c. 12.   [4] 2, 3 Edw. VI. c. 92.
[5] 1 Mar. c. 1.   [6] 5 Eliz. I. c. 17.

and detestable Vice of Buggery aforesaid, to the high displeasure of Almighty God', in consequence of which the statute of 1533 (not, curiously enough, the later and somewhat more satisfactory statute of 1548) was revived, and made to be 'in full force, strength, and effect for ever'.[1]

This Act remained operative for the next two hundred and seventy-five years, during which time there are few other legislative references to homosexual practices. A certain number of General Pardons were issued, but the clemency of the Crown always excepted those who had committed the 'crimes against nature'.[2] In 1823 assault with intent to commit an unnatural offence was made punishable by hard labour and imprisonment in addition to, or in lieu of, fine or imprisonment;[3] and in 1826 sodomy was included among the "infamous crimes", accusation of which by letter, knowingly and wilfully made, rendered the sender thereof guilty of felony.[4]

In 1828 the statute of 1563 was repealed by a consolidating Act which dealt with a large number of offences against the person,[5] but Mr Gordon Westwood is incorrect in stating that the death penalty for sodomy was thereby abolished,[6] for the same Act also provided:

> 9 GEO. IV. c. 31 § 15: ' . . . That every Person convicted of the abominable Crime of Buggery committed either with Mankind or with any Animal, shall suffer death as a Felon.'

A further section dealt with the question of proof that the offence had been committed:

> 9 GEO. IV. c. 31 § 18: '. . . Whereas upon Trials for the crimes of Buggery and of Rape, and of carnally abusing Girls under the respective Ages hereinbefore mentioned Offenders frequently

---

[1] See E. Gibson, op. cit., ii, p. 1082.

[2] 7 Jac. I. c. 24; 12 Car. II. c. 11; 25 Car. II. c. 5; 2 Will. & Mar. c. 10 ; 6, 7 Will. & Mar. c. 20; 7 Ann. c. 22; 3 Geo. I. c. 19; 7 Geo. I. c. 29 are listed in E. Gibson, op. cit., ii, p. 1082.

[3] 3 Geo. IV. c. 114.

[4] See 4 Geo. IV. c. 54 and 6 Geo. IV. c. 19.

[5] 9 Geo. IV. c. 31 § 1.

[6] Op. cit., p. 80.

escape by reason of the "Difficulty of the Proof which has been required of the Completion of those several Crimes"; for Remedy thereof be it enacted, That it shall not be necessary, in any of those cases, to prove the actual Emission of Seed, but that the carnal Knowledge shall be deemed complete upon Proof of Penetration only.'

The removal of the death penalty did not come until 1861, with the passing of the Offences against the Person Act, which laid down that:

24 & 25 VICT. c. 100 § 61: 'Whosoever shall be convicted of the abominable crime of buggery, committed either with mankind or with any animal, shall be liable, at the discretion of the Court, to be kept in penal servitude for life, or for any term not less than ten years.'

24 & 25 VICT. c. 100 § 62: 'Whosoever shall attempt to commit the said abominable crime, or shall be guilty of any assault with intent to commit the same, or of any indecent assault upon any male person, shall be guilty of a misdemeanor, and being convicted thereof shall be liable, at the discretion of the Court, to be kept in penal servitude for any term not exceeding ten years and not less than three years, or to be imprisoned for any term not exceeding two years with or without hard labour.'

Section 63 of the Act again provided that penetration, and not emission, should constitute proof of the offence in question.

The last major piece of legislation against homosexual offences was passed nearly twenty-five years later. In 1885 a Bill was introduced into Parliament 'to make further provision for the protection of women and girls, the suppression of brothels and other purposes'. This Bill passed the Lords and two readings in the Commons without any reference being made to male homosexual practices. Then, at the committee stage, one member (Mr Labouchere) moved the insertion of a new clause dealing with such practices; leave was given by the House for its inclusion, and it was adopted without discussion after Sir Henry James had proposed an amendment increasing the maximum penalty from one year to two.[1] Thus the clause in question became part of the Criminal Law Amendment Act of 1885, and provided that:

> 48 & 49 VICT. c. 69 § 11: 'Any male person who, in public or private, commits or is a party to the commission of, or procures or attempts to procure the commission by any male person of, any act of gross indecency with another male person, shall be guilty of a misdemeanor, and being convicted thereof shall be liable at the discretion of the Court to be imprisoned for any term not exceeding two years, with or without hard labour.'

By this unfortunate enactment male homosexual acts committed in private were for the first time brought within the scope of the criminal law. It is doubtful, as Sir Travers Humphreys says, 'whether the House fully appreciated that the words "in public or private" in the new clause had completely altered the law',[2] and it is not even clear what prompted its addition to a Bill relating to a wholly different matter—unless it was a badly-worded attempt to deal with male as well as female prostitution. For the blackmailer it has proved a lucrative piece of legislation; it has often busied the courts with matters which belong more properly to the moralist, the pastor, and the psychiatrist than to the criminal lawyer; and there is no proof that it has had any marked deterrent or ameliorative effect.

Such, in its broad outlines, is the state of the criminal law in England at present, so far as it relates to male homosexual practices. Sodomy is penalized under the Offences against the Person Act of 1861, and all other forms of homosexual practice— mutual masturbation, inter-femoral connexion, *fellatio,* and so forth—under the Criminal Law Amendment Act of 1885. A few slight amendments and modifications have been made in the application and operation of the sections of these Acts dealing with homosexual offences, but the general character of the law has remained unchanged.

---

[1] See *Hansard,* vol. 300, coll. 1397–1398 for the proceedings of the House in this connexion.

[2] See H. M. Hyde, *The Trials of Oscar Wilde* (London, 1948), p. 6.

VII

CONCLUSION

THE purpose of this study has been to examine the historical and theological factors which have contributed to the formation of the traditional Western Christian attitude to homosexual practices —an attitude epitomized by Blackstone when he wrote that the 'crime against nature' was one which 'the voice of nature and of reason, and the express law of God, determine to be capital. Of which we have a signal instance, long before the Jewish dispensation, by the destruction of two cities by fire from heaven; so that this is an universal, not merely a provincial precept'.[1]

Blackstone's words draw attention to two important features in the development of this tradition—the 'express law of God', and the 'signal instance' of the overthrow of Sodom and Gomorrah. In the Old Testament the Law condemns sodomists (and possibly other homosexual offenders) to death as perpetrators of an abomination against the Lord, while in the New Testament they are denounced as transgressors of the natural order, and are disinherited from the kingdom of God as followers of the vile practices of the heathen. The reinterpretation of the Sodom story at the hands of the Pseudepigraphists, Josephus, and Philo was immediately accepted by the Christian Church and has remained authoritative and virtually unchallenged until now— teaching that those who indulge in unnatural vice may bring upon themselves and upon all who tolerate their depravity the fearful vengeance of God. Together, the Bible and Sodom have exercised a powerful influence upon the thought and the imagination of the

---

[1] Op. cit., iv., p. 215.

West in the matter of homosexual practices, and the effect of this
is to be seen in the tradition of which we have attempted to trace
the growth.

Early Christian opinion and canon law denounced chiefly the
paidiophthoros or *stuprator puerorum*—the pæderast who was
addicted to the "love for boys" which was so characteristic a
feature of sexual life in the society of the Hellenistic decadence.
Roman law likewise concerned itself with the protection of *pueri
prætextati* or minors, but it also penalized the male homosexual
prostitute, the active sodomist, and the procurer, while in his
novellæ Justinian condemned all who 'practise among themselves
the most disgraceful lusts'—a phrase capable of very wide interpretation. The edict of Theodosius, Valentinian, and Arcadius
gave statutory expression to the opinion of the pagan jurists that
sodomy is a capital crime, and bequeathed to succeeding ages the
penalty of the *vindices flammæ* as a means of execution. But it is
doubtful whether this mode of punishment, preserved in the
systems of mediæval customary law which had been influenced
by the Theodosian Code, was often inflicted; in England, at any
rate, it seems to have remained in abeyance.

In the Middle Ages, though the Crown was entitled to take
independent action, the Church exercised a general jurisdiction
over homosexual offenders, and imposed its own spiritual discipline upon those whom its courts convicted. At an earlier date
confessors sought the guidance of the Penitentials, which were
remarkable for their detailed analyses of homosexual acts; their
commendable attempts to distinguish offences according to the
gravity of each, and to assign proportionate punishment, might
profitably have been heeded in later times. Generally speaking,
the mediævals displayed a greater awareness than their predecessors of the complexity of sexual behaviour and the difficulty
of assessing the morality of sexual acts; but this did not affect their
final conclusion that all homosexual practices, being *peccata contra
naturam*, are mortally sinful. The English law, on the other hand,
ventured upon no such nice distinctions, and until the passing of
the Act of 1885 took cognizance only of sodomy, which it

treated for over three hundred years as a felony punishable by death.

So far as the evidence before us will permit, we must now attempt some evaluation of the tradition which has been described, and by which legislation has been sanctioned and public opinion governed in Britain. Does careful exegesis and historical enquiry show that it is a sound tradition which can still be accepted unreservedly as a reliable guide in all matters relating to sexual inversion; or must we seek elsewhere (as some insist) for the principles according to which one of the gravest moral problems of our time should be handled? These questions have already been partly answered by some of the conclusions stated in the course of our enquiry.

The most prominent feature in the tradition proves on examination to be the most vulnerable. It has always been accepted without question that God declared his judgement upon homosexual practices once and for all time by the destruction of the cities of the Plain. But Sodom and Gomorrah, as we have seen, actually have nothing whatever to do with such practices; the interpretation of the Sodom story generally received by Western Christendom turns out to be nothing more than a post-Exilic Jewish reinterpretation devised and exploited by patriotic rigorists for polemical purposes. Thus disappears the assumption that an act of Divine retribution in the remote past has relieved us of the responsibility for making an assessment of homosexual acts in terms of theological and moral principles. It is no longer permissible to take refuge in the contention that God himself pronounced these acts "detestable and abominable" above every other sexual sin, nor to explain natural catastrophes and human disasters as his vengeance upon those who indulge in them. It is much to be hoped that we shall soon hear the last of Sodom and Gomorrah in connexion with homosexual practices—though doubtless the term "sodomy" will always remain as a reminder of the unfortunate consequences which have attended the reinterpretation of an ancient story in the interests of propaganda.

Having dismissed Sodom and Gomorrah as irrelevant to our

enquiry, let us turn to the rest of the Scriptural material relating to homosexual practices. There are six places in the Bible where such practices are plainly condemned, and we must now ask to what extent the passages in question bear directly or indirectly upon our approach to, and handling of, modern problems. From the Old Testament, it must be admitted, we receive little help. Although the laws in the Holiness Code of Leviticus refer to 'lying with mankind as with womankind', the meaning of this phrase is ambiguous. All that can be said with any assurance is that it must at any rate include sodomy, which one law forbids as an abomination to the Lord, and another punishes as a capital offence; but whether or not it also relates to other acts must remain a matter for conjecture. A more humane, if not more enlightened jurisprudence has already rejected the death penalty for sodomists, and these simple enactments, framed with reference to a situation so different from our own (if, indeed, they are not merely "abstract" items of legislation), give us no guidance in dealing with the manifold and complex problems of sexual inversion. They stand as a witness to the conviction shared by the ancient Hebrews with other contemporary peoples that homosexual practices are peculiarly disreputable, and deserve exemplary punishment as unnatural indulgences, incompatible with the vocation and moral obligations of the People of God. This view may not greatly assist the legislator or the sociologist for whom the sanctions of religion are not absolute, but it cannot be lightly dismissed by the Church—although it may eventually need some qualification by the moral theologian in the light of further scientific discovery and of a reconsideration of the morality of sexual acts as a whole.

St Paul likewise denounces homosexual practices as inconsistent with membership of the kingdom of God, but our knowledge of life in the social underworld of the first century enables us to set his words in their correct context. He specifically mentions the *arsenokoitai* or active sodomists, and the *malakoi* or passive sodomists (who were often prostitutes or *exsoleti*), both of whom are familiar enough from the pages of Petronius and others; and it can hardly be doubted that he also had such types in mind when writing to the Romans of those men who, 'leaving the natural use of the woman, burned in their lust one toward another, men with men working unseemliness'—the last, a phrase sufficiently wide in meaning to cover every kind of homosexual indulgence practised by the vicious in that or any other age. Although St Paul does not expressly refer to corrupters of youth or *paidophthoroi*, we may be certain that he intended his condemnations to include them.

Here, then, we have decisive Biblical authority for censuring the conduct of those whom we may describe as male perverts, such as the depraved pæderasts and catamites of the *Satyricon*; but do the Apostle's strictures apply also to the homosexual acts of the genuine invert, and in particular to those physical expressions of affection which may take place between two persons of the same sex who affirm that they are "in love"? To such situations it can hardly be said that the New Testament speaks, since the condition of inversion, with all its special problems, was quite unknown at that time. Nor does it assist us in the delicate matter of assigning punishment to those who have committed homosexual acts in circumstances of which the criminal law must necessarily take account—that is to say, acts involving violence, public indecency, or corruption of the young. Such matters, declares the author of the first Epistle to Timothy, belong to the province of the temporal magistrate; but he does not even suggest what principles ought to guide those responsible for the administration of justice, so as to ensure that for each offence an appropriate and equitable penalty is imposed.

As we survey the development of this tradition it becomes evident that the effect of the reinterpreted Sodom story upon the mind of the Church was in fact more profound than that of either the Levitical laws or the teaching of the New Testament. Both of these (and especially St Paul's words in the Epistle to the Romans) were often used to emphasize the lesson drawn from Genesis xix, but the latter had the most powerful influence of all upon the fears and imagination of the Christian West. It is, of

course, futile to speculate whether the Western attitude would
have been different had it been realized that Sodom and Gomorrah
had no bearing upon the question of homosexual practices. It
might, for instance, be argued that in such an event the legislation
of the Theodosian Code would have been altogether less severe.
But this would involve the gratuitous assumption that the provisions of the two statutes of Constantius and Constans, and of
Theodosius, Valentinian, and Arcadius, were largely determined
by the belief that these cities had been destroyed on account of
their sodomy. It is well, therefore, not to forget that in these laws
the Theodosian Code expresses not only the spirit of the Levitical
enactments against homosexual practices, but also (and this is
more directly relevant) the consensus of opinion among the great
lawyers of the third century—who were not, of course, Christians.
There is no doubt that prior to the time of Constantine Roman
jurisprudence had been moving steadily towards the conclusion
that sodomy ought to be regarded as a capital crime, especially
when it involved assault or the corruption of a boy under age; and
we may suppose not unreasonably that this conviction, supported
by the legislation of the Holiness Code, would have gained
general acceptance in Christendom in the absence of any independent confirmation purporting to come from the reinterpreted
Sodom story.

Both the Bible and the Roman law encouraged a severe treatment of sodomy, but there was also a mitigating influence, partly
theological and partly ecclesiastical in character, which has usually
been overlooked. Justinian, in his edicts, had insisted that homosexual acts were sins as well as crimes, and that the penalties of the
secular law were only to be invoked against the obdurate and
the unrepentant—and there is a strange irony in the fact that the
emperor who sought to temper judgement with mercy has often
been blamed for inculcating an attitude which derives chiefly from
the harsher rigour of the Theodosian Code. During the Middle
Ages the principle enunciated by the great legist found expression
in the practice of the reservation of homosexual offences for trial
and sentence in the Church courts, and this led (in England at

least) to the virtual desuetude of capital punishment at the hands of the civil power. Thus the Act of 1533, which brought sodomists under the jurisdiction of the secular magistracy and reasserted the death penalty, was a retrograde step which even the Act of 1861 did not wholly reverse; while the Act of 1885, which treated as criminal offences any homosexual acts committed in private by adult and consenting male persons, transferred to the cognizance of the temporal courts certain sexual sins which lie within the competence of none but a spiritual tribunal. To this extent it may be said that the English (and latterly, the British) law represents a regrettable departure from the developed Western tradition of mediæval times.

It must not be forgotten that Sodom and Gomorrah, the legislation and injunctions of the Bible, and the Roman law, were (so to speak) only the proximate or immediate determinants of the traditional Western view of homosexual practices—those which most readily lend themselves to historical investigation. Underlying them, without doubt, are various socio-psychological factors which still await full and careful examination. Among these factors must certainly be included the cultural attitudes described by Mr G. Rattray Taylor in his book *Sex in History*, where he contrasts the patrist society—repressive, authoritarian, conservative, strongly subordinationist in its view of woman, and horrified at homosexual practices, with the matrist society— liberal, enquiring, democratic, inclined to enhance the status of woman, and tolerant of homosexual practices.[1] His thesis is that the pattern of family life and parent-child relationship typical of any generation will naturally tend to reproduce itself in the character and outlook of the succeeding generation by inducing, in the majority of individuals comprising the latter, a father- or mother-identification, as the case may be; and that the resultant identity of attitude perpetuated from one generation to another leads to the establishment of a culture which is itself either patrist or matrist. He concludes that the tradition of the Christian West

---

[1] See especially Ch. iv, pp. 72 ff.

has always been fundamentally patrist—a view which is certainly confirmed in large measure by our survey of the historical facts relating to homosexual practices; but the theory as a whole still awaits full examination. It is likely that when enquiry is made into this and cognate questions, much light may be thrown upon what is at present perplexing, obscure, and apparently irrational in contemporary sexual ideas and attitudes. In particular, it may explain the reason for the curious disparity between the moral judgement passed upon adultery and fornication on the one hand, and sodomy and homosexual acts in general on the other—and for the horror with which the latter are so often regarded. Such an enquiry, however, lies outside the scope of this study. When it can be undertaken it may well prove both illuminating and disturbing; meanwhile, it is necessary to bear constantly in mind as we consider the problem of homosexuality how little we know as yet about the deep-seated psychological factors, social as well as personal, which determine our sexual attitudes.

A better understanding of such factors will undoubtedly help to explain certain striking anomalies in the tradition which has affected so profoundly our laws and public opinion in regard to homosexual practices. Perhaps the most remarkable of these anomalies is the almost complete disregard of sexual acts committed by women with one another—of the practices variously termed lesbianism, tribadism, and sapphism. In the Epistle to the Romans, St Paul condemns the pagan women who 'changed the natural use into that which is against nature'—a phrase which is ambiguous, but which ought probably to be taken (as John Chrysostom takes it) as directed against lesbianism. The Penitentials punish tribadism, including the use of the artificial phallus; councils at Paris in 1212 and at Rouen in 1214 prohibit nuns from sleeping together; and there is no doubt that the *concubitus ad non debitum sexum* which Aquinas includes among the species of *vitium contra naturam* relates to female no less than to male homosexual acts. But these, and a few other references of similar import, some of which have not been discussed in this study, more or less exhaust the allusions to lesbianism in theology and ecclesiastical legislation prior to the Reformation; and it is ignored by both mediæval and modern law—except, presumably, by the latter in cases of indecent assault.

Why have homosexual acts been penalized so heavily (and sometimes, in our own day, so savagely) when committed by men, while at the same time they have been virtually disregarded when committed by women? This strange and illogical (and, indeed, grossly unjust) state of affairs cannot fully be explained until we understand more than we do at present about the psychological factors which help to determine our social attitudes, but the historical study of sexual ideas throws some light upon the problem. In particular, it suggests that at certain points there is a significant connexion between the traditional Western views of homosexuality and homosexual practices on the one hand, and of woman and marriage on the other, and that these two questions, though apparently unrelated, must not be isolated one from the other.

At various stages in our enquiry we have already encountered the notion that in male homosexual acts, and especially in sodomy, there is something peculiarly degrading or disgusting. In regard to this revulsion of feeling two points deserve notice: first, that it is never attributed directly to the fact that sodomy, at any rate, involves copulation *per anum*—a mode of sexual indulgence which is by no means uncommon in heterosexual relationships; and secondly, that it is a reaction more characteristic of men than of women, who often exhibit a commendable open-mindedness and sympathy towards the invert and his or her problems. When male homosexual acts are considered *per se,* and with a mind free (as far as that is possible) from emotional prejudices, it cannot be said that they are intrinsically either more or less reprehensible than lesbian practices. Hence the reason for the traditional discrimination against the former and disregard of the latter must be sought elsewhere than in the nature of male homosexual acts as such.

Both the terminology used with reference to male practices, and the assumptions underlying the attitude of society, are

M

revealing. There has been a marked tendency to regard sodomy in particular as though it were, so to speak, "playing the woman" to another man, or using another man "like a woman", according to whether the part taken was passive or active. In other words, this act has been looked upon as one which involves the degradation, not so much of human nature itself as of the male, since in it he simulates or encourages or compels another to simulate the coital function of the female—a "perversion" intolerable in its implications to any society organized in accordance with the theory that woman is essentially subordinate to man. Thus in certain androcentric cultures, and especially that of the Christian West, a man who acted "like a woman" was treated as one who had betrayed not only himself but his whole sex, dragging his fellows down with him in his voluntary disgrace; while the active sodomist, being implicated in this reversal of "nature" (that is, of androcentricity), was equally reviled. And there is no doubt that despite the emancipation of woman and its far-reaching consequences, something of this deep-seated but irrational view of woman remains today to influence the attitude of men in general towards the homosexual male—whether or not he actually indulges in sodomy or other homosexual acts. The lesbian's practices, on the other hand, do not imply any lowering of her personal or sexual status, and can be ignored by a society which is still in some respects fundamentally androcentric. To "corrupt" a younger girl by initiating her into the pleasures of tribadism is thought trivial compared with the "corruption" of a youth by "making a woman" of him, or inciting him to inflict such a degradation upon a fellow man; while on a wholly different level of human intercourse convention has decreed that women, but not men, may display affection for one another, or may live together without suspicion. It might perhaps be well for us frankly to face the fact that rationalization of sexual prejudices, animated by false notions of sexual privilege, has played no inconsiderable part in forming the tradition which we have inherited, and probably controls opinion and policy today in the matter of homosexuality to a greater extent than is commonly realized.

Another reason for the distinction traditionally made between male and female homosexual practices is undoubtedly the fact that only the former involve seminal emission.[1] To understand this, it is necessary to appreciate the remarkable influence exerted upon our sexual attitudes (and, indeed, upon our theology) by what can only be described as a superstitious reverence for semen, which had its origin in antiquity, and in an ignorance of human physiology which happily no longer exists. The ancients had no knowledge of the process of ovulation in woman, nor of the way in which conception occurs. According to the medical philosophers, the embryo was concocted from semen and menstrual fluid; but the woman's contribution was confined to the provision of a suitable place in which this mixture could coagulate into the fœtus. She was little more than a well-equipped incubator in which the seed was deposited by means of coitus there is no difference, declares Galen, between sowing the womb and sowing the earth.[2] In his view, semen is comparable to the seeds of plants; it possesses all its faculties from the beginning and has, in effect, the attributes of the fertilized ovum.[3] It is a distillation from the body, explains Aristotle—the quintessence of useful nutriment, refined into its highest form;[4] and from it the human being is formed. Potentially it has a sentient soul; but the menstrual fluid only contains potentially the parts of the body, and a nutritive soul.[5] Fully acquainted with the science of their day, the Christian Fathers express the same views,[6] which Clement of Alexandria epitomizes in the statement that semen is *met' oligon anthrōpon*—something almost, or about to become, a man.[7]

---

[1] This is not affected by the fact that 9 Geo. IV. c. 31 § 18 and 24 & 25 Vict. c. 100 § 63 stipulated that penetration, not ejaculation, constitutes proof of homosexual "carnal knowledge".

[2] *De fac. nat.* i. 6. [3] Ibid., ii. 3.

[4] *De gen. animal.* i. 18. [5] Ibid., ii. 3.

[6] Cf. Pacian, *de bapt.* 7; *Recog. Clem.* viii. 26, 28, 32; Athenagoras, *de res.* 17; John Chrysostom, *in I Cor. hom.* xvii. 2, xli. 2; *in I Thess. hom.* vii. 2; *in epist. ad Hebr. hom.* xxiii. 2; Augustine, *de bon. conj.* 20; *de civ. Dei,* xiv. 23; *de nupt. et concup.* ii. 29; *de anima,* iv. 6 (v); *de Trin.* xii. 6, xv. 27.

[7] *Pæd.* 10.

This conception of semen as a substance "almost human" overshadowed the sexual thought, not only of antiquity, but of the whole Western world until the sixteenth century, and has left its mark upon our own ideas of sexual conduct and morality. It has undoubtedly been responsible in no small measure for the fact that society has always tended to reprobate and punish the homosexual practices of males while more or less ignoring those of females, since the latter, involving no "waste" of the precious fluid, could be dismissed as mere feminine lewdness. It is no longer possible, however, to maintain this distinction between male and female homosexual acts, for the ancient theory of the nature of semen and of human conception has long ago been rendered obsolete by medical science, and with its passing the idea of woman as primarily a breeding machine has also disappeared— though the profound and extensive cultural consequences of these notions have not yet been entirely dissipated. Their subtle influence upon the attitudes which we unconsciously assume makes it necessary to guard against the temptation to perpetuate a meaningless double moral standard in regard to homosexual practices. There can be no rational defence of the legal and social discrimination between the sexes in this matter—but this does not mean that the sodomist must be allowed the freedom and immunity from punishment now accorded to the lesbian; rather, it seems logical to claim that in the case of each the criminal law should take cognizance only of acts involving assault or violence, the corruption of minors, and public indecency or nuisance. Justice and equity can demand no less and exact no more than parity of treatment between men and women in the matter of homosexual offences.

Not unconnected with the question just discussed is the further anomaly that homosexual acts between males have commonly been condemned more severely than heterosexual immorality. Resort to a prostitute or indulgence in other kinds of fornication did at least proclaim a man's essential virility; and although he might thereby incur the censure of the moralist, he never earned the contempt of his fellows as he would have done by "acting the woman", or by imposing upon others of his own sex the unspeakable degradation of "effeminacy". Even the adulterer, despite the condemnations of religion and the penalties of the law, was usually less harshly regarded by a society which reserved for the cuckolded husband a ridicule stronger than its disapprobation of the successful paramour.

Something of the same paradoxical attitude survives today in the relative contemporary estimates of homosexual and hetero- sexual immorality. The dissolution in 1947 of some sixty thousand marriages; a divorce rate which seems to remain more or less static at an annual figure of around thirty thousand; a pre- marital and extra-marital conception rate of approximately one maternity in eight—these are undoubtedly all matters of the gravest concern to responsible persons, but they have excited no general outcry comparable to the somewhat hysterical demonstra- tions of moral indignation which have lately been directed against the male homosexual. Yet such statistics, and others bearing upon birth and matrimony, veil a picture of folly and selfishness, of wrecked homes and broken hearts, and above all, of misery and harm and wrong inflicted upon innocent children, in comparison with which the volume and seriousness of homosexual offences (even including those committed with minors) appears relatively trivial. In the face of such a picture it is incredible that there should still be those who maintain the quixotic contention that the practising male homosexual does more harm than the person who seduces a husband or wife and breaks up a marriage, who assaults and injures a young girl, or who begets and then dis- claims responsibility for an illegitimate child. The homosexual corruption of a boy (and, for that matter, of a girl—though of this the law takes no account) is undeniably a grave offence; but a sense of reality and proportion seems to be wanting in those who represent male homosexual offences (including those committed in private by consenting adults) as immeasurably the worst of social evils. Moreover, it is not generally appreciated that while a male homosexual is rarely responsible for the disruption of a union, cases not infrequently come to light in which a wife has been seduced by a female homosexual, or in which an unhealthy and obviously homosexual attachment between a wife and another woman has caused a marriage to founder.

In his Epistle to the Romans, St Paul wrote that homosexual practices brought upon those who indulged in them 'that recompense of their error which was due'. Augustine, as we have seen,[1] interpreted this as meaning that such practices are not only sinful *per se,* but are also a requital for other sins; that is to say, their very existence is evidence of the nexus between cause and effect in the moral realm which the Apostle described by that often misunderstood term, the "wrath of God". This conception of homosexual practices as a "recompense for error" is doubly significant.

In any society the extent of homosexual practice and perversion is always one of the more striking indications of a general corruption or defect in its sexual life. Thus the so-called "problem of homosexuality" which confronts us today is really a problem arising from the decay of moral standards and the abandonment of moral responsibility in the field of heterosexual relation—both, in their turn, the result of false or imperfect conceptions of the nature of sex, and of ignorance or rejection of the will of God for man and woman. Homosexual perversion, therefore, is not itself a fount of corrupting influence, but only, as it were, the ineluctable consequence of a corrosion which has already left its mark upon marriage and family life and, if not checked, may ultimately undermine the whole social order and lead to sexual anarchy. Consequently any attempt to suppress homosexual practices by the rigour of the criminal law is merely a feeble effort to cure symptoms while neglecting the disease which has produced them. Despite what may seem at times to be almost an attitude of complacent indifference to its condition, there is little doubt that our society is aware of the nature of this disease, and that it has at bottom a profoundly uneasy conscience on that score. But sooner or later an unpalatable truth must be faced: instead of addressing

---

[1] See above, p. 11.

itself energetically to the reform of all that is amiss in its sexual life and ideas, it has attempted to relieve its sense of guilt by turning upon the male homosexual as a convenient scape-goat. Such a projection of blame is, of course, ultimately futile; but much distress, harm, and injustice may be caused before it can be effectively exposed as a discreditable evasion of responsibility. Augustine suggests that whatever may be said of the intrinsic morality of homosexual practices, they are certainly a "recompense" with which any society is likely to be visited when it departs from the Divine principles by which human life should be governed, and from the allegiance which it owes to God; and that they always point to a radical disorganization, if not corruption, of the relationships between men and women upon which the whole social structure is reared.

This "recompense", however, may also take a form which must be carefully distinguished from any homosexual perversions in which it may manifest itself. At present we know all too little about the ætiology of sexual inversion, but there can be no doubt that this mysterious and unfortunate condition illustrates in a remarkable way the visitation of the sins of the fathers upon the children. In many cases it appears to be due to an unsatisfactory relationship between a child and its parents, or to the repercussion upon a child of some grave defect or maladjustment in the relationship between its father and mother. Comparatively little thought seems to have been given to the possibility that marital disharmony, divorce, and the disruption of family life by war (to mention only three factors) may cause an apparently incurable deflection of the sexual impulse leading sometimes (though not necessarily, nor in every case) either to habitual indulgence in homosexual practices as "normal" in those so conditioned, or to the commission of some "offence" in a moment of personal stress or crisis. The genuine invert is often, so to speak, a by-product of the sin of a previous generation, and receives as a "recompense" of the error of others an affliction which closes the door to marriage and family life, gives rise to exceptional difficulties of personal adjustment, and involves both an isolation and temptations unknown to the heterosexual. Society, therefore, has a heavy responsibility towards the inverts whom it creates by its relational failures and its wars, and should abandon the illusion that its uneasy conscience can be quieted by hollow displays of self-righteous indignation, by ostracism of the homosexual, or by campaigns against "vice". Again, the only solution is to attack the problem at its root—to deal with the social and sexual evils in which the condition of inversion frequently originates. Promotion of good marriages and happy homes will achieve a result immeasurably greater and more valuable than punitive legislation aimed at the private practices of adult homosexuals, while the adulterer and adulteress are allowed to pursue their anti-social designs unchecked.

The question of sexual inversion takes us from the anomalies in the Western tradition to its deficiencies as a guide to the handling of modern problems. While the compilers of the Penitentials and the mediæval theologians attempted to distinguish between different kinds of homosexual practice and different types of homosexual offender, neither they nor their predecessors were aware of the broad distinction which psychology has compelled us to make between those whom we have termed respectively the invert and the pervert. To Aquinas as to St Paul, indulgence in homosexual acts proclaimed a person to be a depraved and vicious "sinner against nature" whose base desires afforded an incontestable proof of moral obliquity. This conviction underlies the entire Western tradition in regard to homosexual practices, but it requires considerable modification in the light of scientific discoveries, and of clinical and other studies. The homosexual pattern is being increasingly revealed as one of bewildering complexity which defies all attempts at classification according to rigid and pre-determined notions. Nevertheless it has at least been established beyond controversy that in many cases sexual inversion is an inherent and apparently unalterable condition—though its causes and character still need careful and detailed investigation.

This condition is in itself morally neutral; but it may find expression in specific homosexual acts—and upon such acts a moral judgement must be passed. What principles ought to direct our moral judgements upon the sexual conduct of the genuine invert? Ought his acts to be regarded precisely as if they were the acts of a pervert? Here the Christian tradition affords us little guidance, for it knows only one kind of homosexual behaviour— that which would be termed perversion; thus to one of the most perplexing ethical problems of our time it has at best but an indirect and dubious relevance. Even the admirably temperate and thorough consideration of homosexual acts by Aquinas[1] is governed by the assumptions typical of his age, and is consequently of limited value where true inversion is concerned. For instance, he treats such acts as a form of *vitium contra naturam*— and the very phrase begs a large and pertinent question which may not be brushed aside.

The male invert, whether practising or not, generally maintains that homosexual acts are, for him, entirely "natural", and that coitus with a woman would be nothing less than a perversion. Hence he would claim that it is unjust and illogical to deny him, should he so desire, the right to express himself and to seek physical satisfaction and relief in acts appropriate to his condition —provided no harm accrues to society or to any individual as a result. Such acts, he would assert, are not "unnatural" simply because the dominant heterosexual majority regards them as "unnatural". It is easy, of course, to refute this contention by an appeal to objective conceptions of the "natural", but it can hardly be gainsaid that there is an obvious, and indeed intrinsic difference between the acts of the pervert and those of the invert—and that the argument of the latter, though patently subjective, is not without a certain plausibility. Faced with the novel and delicate responsibility of making an assessment of the invert's behaviour which does justice both to his abnormal condition and the personal problems which it creates, and to the claims of morality, we find that our tradition gives us no assistance. Nor does it help us

---

[1] See above, pp. 115 f.

to determine what view to take of inversion itself, for it is wholly unaware of the existence of such a state arising from causes outside the subject's control.

Before bringing this study to a close, several historical points deserve brief comment. Our investigations will at least have demonstrated plainly how necessary it is to exercise caution when drawing, from the meagre and uncertain data in our possession, conclusions regarding the incidence of homosexual practices in the past. Misinterpretation of conciliar enactments, civil legislation, and the recordings of chroniclers has often led to the construction of an entirely erroneous picture of the extent of "homosexuality", both at particular periods, and generally throughout the history of the West. It is advisable, therefore, to accept with considerable reserve some of the confident assertions upon the subject which have been made by writers in the past, especially since some of them have tended to handle their material with a polemical bias. The truth is that when the evidence has been sifted and evaluated, we find that we know all too little about the matter.

Many examples of such errors have already been given, and another may be added. Mr Gordon Westwood writes: 'The homosexual activities of Edward II resulted in his murder in 1327. According to Higden, "He was sleyne with a hoote broche putte thro the secret place posteriale" '.[1] It is remarkable that Mr Westwood, and others who have permitted themselves a like inference from Higden's report of the mode of this sovereign's death, should have been unaware that the chronicler's veracity was challenged by Mr S. A. Moore over sixty years ago. In an exhaustive study of the question, he shows that there is very strong ground for discounting the tradition of Edward's murder as something *vulgariter dictum*, and suggests with much plausibility that his death was probably due to poison.[2]

Such reliable records as we possess refer exclusively to homosexual *practices*, and almost exclusively to *male* practices; they tell

---

[1] Op. cit., p. 101; cf. *Polychronicon Ranulphi Higden* (Rolls Series, vol. viii, 1882).
[2] See S. A. Moore, "Documents relating to the death and burial of King Edward II", in *Antiquity*, vol. I, pp. 215–226, 1887.

us nothing about "homosexuality" itself—that is to say, about the condition of inversion, and virtually nothing about lesbianism. Statements concerning the prevalence of inversion, therefore, are speculative and practically valueless. Indications, for instance, that sodomy was frequent at any particular time might suggest that perversion was common, but they would not warrant the inference that inverts were plentiful. Thus it is often asserted that "homosexuality" was almost an institution in ancient Greece— which is, in fact, nonsense, for an inherent condition such as inversion cannot be institutionalized. What is really meant by this statement is that in certain Greek communities male homosexual relationships between a youth and an older man were idealized, and seem to have been an accepted feature of the upbringing at least of boys of good social standing. In practice, there is no doubt that this custom led to indulgence in sexual acts; but neither *paiderastia* nor the *paidophthoria* into which it rapidly degenerated afford any evidence that the true male invert was more than usually common among the Greeks, whose men generally married and became fathers, and were not averse from heterosexual pleasures such as those of prostitution and hetairism.

Nevertheless, it is undeniable that at certain times and in certain societies homosexual relationships and practices appear to have been exceptionally prevalent. This may admittedly have been due sometimes to a temporary increase in the incidence of actual inversion, due to social causes; but a study of homosexual practice suggests that a more likely explanation is to be found in the fact that sexual fashions, like others, change from time to time, and that there will always be found not a few who will easily conform to the vogue of the moment. Human beings, as we have already observed, are sexually very adaptable and accommodating whenever conventional, religious, or moral restraints do not inhibit their conduct; and men in particular are inclined to be adventurous and experimentative. The court of William Rufus affords a striking example of this capacity, but it is no less evident in cases where there is an enforced segregation from the complementary sex due to imprisonment or service with the armed forces; while on a vaster scale the *paiderastia* and subsequent *paidophthoria* of the Greeks shows how a civilization can adopt and sometimes regularize homosexual relationships and practices. The causes which produce such fashions in sexual conduct require further investigation, but of the fashions themselves there can be no doubt—and recognition of this fact may well throw considerable light upon certain aspects of the modern homosexuality problem.

Enough has been said in the foregoing pages to vindicate the Church against the common imputation that ecclesiastical prejudice and fanaticism has been mainly responsible for the harsh attitude of the law and public opinion towards the male homosexual offender. The Church's critics generally trace the provisions and the spirit of the present legislation through the mediæval canon law to the edicts of Justinian, and thence to their origin in the enactments of Leviticus. In fact, however, the ancestry of the current British law goes back more evidently to the Henrician statute of 1533, the Theodosian Code, and the jurisprudence of the pagan lawyers of third-century Rome. Although he was undoubtedly influenced by Leviticus, the Sodom story, and the jurists, Justinian must be given credit for introducing in his *novellæ* the Christian principle of setting mercy and forgiveness before the infliction of criminal punishment; and the Church, following his example, imposed spiritual penalties and discipline upon the sinner, but rarely delivered him into the hands of the civil magistrate. It was only when the jurisdiction of the ecclesiastical courts over the homosexual offender was transferred to the temporal authority that clemency yielded to rigour and the capital sentence prescribed by the Theodosian Code was revived to requite the new felony.

It now remains only to state briefly the conclusions to which this study of "homosexuality" in the Western Christian tradition points.

1. It is evident that this tradition is

    (a) erroneous, in so far as it represents the destruction of Sodom and Gomorrah as a Divine judgement upon homosexual practices, such as ought to determine both the attitude of society to the homosexual offender, and the punishment inflicted upon him by the law; whereas this story, in fact, has no relevance to the matter in question.

(b) defective, in that

(i) it is ignorant of inversion as a *condition* due to biological, psychological, or genetical causes; and consequently of the distinction between the invert and the pervert. Therefore,

(ii) it assumes that all homosexual acts are, so to speak, "acts of perversion"—a term which does not happily or accurately describe the acts to which the invert may be impelled by his condition.

(iii) it takes very little account of female homosexuality, and makes a wholly unwarranted discrimination between the sodomist and the lesbian.

(iv) it unjustifiably regards male homosexual offences as both intrinsically and socially more serious than heterosexual offences, such as seduction of young girls by men, fornication in general, and above all, adultery.

(v) it tends to think too exclusively in terms of the act of sodomy.

(vi) by maintaining for so long (at least in theory) that homosexual acts, and especially sodomy, merited capital punishment, it has encouraged the imposition of disproportionately severe penalties upon the homosexual offender.

(vii) it is by no means entirely a tradition founded and built upon reason, for it has been strongly influenced by emotional and psychological factors into which enquiry needs to be made.

For these reasons the tradition can no longer be regarded as an adequate guide by the theologian, the legislator, the sociologist, and the magistrate. Moreover, it has latterly been subjected, as we have seen, to various interpretations displaying an anti-ecclesiastical or anti-Christian bias, which have in fact obscured certain of its important features, and have represented it as in some particulars quite other than it actually is. Nevertheless,

2. The tradition has several positive features of great value which we must affirm:

(a) it emphasizes the duty of the law to protect the young.

(b) it bears witness to the principle, overlaid in the English law since the Reformation, that the homosexual offender is not only a criminal who may deserve punishment, but also a sinner who needs to be won to repentance; and that justice must therefore be tempered with mercy.

(c) it affords useful guidance as to the treatment of perversion and the pervert.

3. A study of this kind naturally suggests points at which legal and other reforms are desirable.

(a) perhaps the most urgently necessary reform is in the law. Here two matters demand action:

(i) legal discrimination between different types of homosexual acts should be abolished, and no account should be taken by the law of such acts when committed in private by consenting adults.

(ii) some of the maximum penalties at present laid down need amendment in accordance with the dictates of humanity, and in order to introduce a general consistency into the punishment of sexual offences as a whole.

(b) no less clamant is the need to remove the anomalies connected with female homosexual practices. There is no theological, practical, or equitable reason why the law should penalize a man for what a woman may do with impunity. Of private homosexual acts by consenting adults of either sex no legal cognizance should be taken, unless violence or fraud are involved; but in the case of offences against minors, of infringement of public decency, and of assault, both men and women should be dealt with equally and impartially.

(c) steps also should be taken to abolish the inconsistencies as between the punishment of homosexual and heterosexual offences. It is manifestly contrary to public policy and the common good that homosexual acts should be so severely penalized, while the adulterer and the adulteress, and those responsible for bringing illegitimate children into the world, stand outside the sanctions of the law.

4. Probably the best way to effect the more urgent of these reforms would be:

(a) to repeal §§ 61 and 62 of the Offences against the Person Act, 1861, and § 11 of the Criminal Law Amendment Act, 1885.

(b) to abandon the legal use of "buggery", and of all such ambiguous terms as "indecent assault", "gross indecency", "unnatural offences", and the like; and to substitute for them the simple and unobjectionable expression, "homosexual act or acts".

(c) to introduce legislation penalizing any male or female person who commits, or attempts to commit, or is a party to the commission of, or procures or attempts to procure the commission by any person of, any homosexual act or acts,

(i) with a person under the legal "age of consent". [Although the present legal "age of consent" is sixteen years, it is desirable that the "age of consent" for both sexes should as soon as possible be brought into conformity with the provisions of the Children's and Young Persons Act, 1933, by being raised to seventeen years]; or

(ii) in circumstances constituting a public nuisance, or an infringement of public decency; or

(iii) involving assault, violence, fraud, or duress.

(d) to ensure that in assessing the penalty due for the commission of any such offence, proper regard is paid to the physical and psychological condition of the offender; and that spiritual counsel and medical and psychiatric treatment is secured in all cases where these are recommended by competent advice.

5. Finally, there are certain matters to which attention ought urgently to be directed:

(a) undoubtedly the most important of all is the promotion of happy marriages and family life, so reducing the incidence of inversion due to psychological causes arising from mal-adjusted relations between husband and wife, and between parents and children.

(b) much study needs to be given to the causes and the nature of the condition of inversion, to the possibility of a "cure" in certain cases, and to the means by which the invert can be helped to accept his abnormality, and to take his place as a useful and fully accepted member of society. This requires in turn,

(c) the education of the public to a sense of understanding and responsibility for the men and women who labour under this peculiar handicap, and the dissipation of prejudices and false ideas regarding the homosexual condition.

INDEX

N